Originally published as *Catherine Breillat: Je ne crois qu'en moi. Entretien avec Murielle Joudet*. Copyright © Capricci 2023.

Published by Semiotext(e)
PO BOX 629, South Pasadena, CA 91031
www.semiotexte.com

Cover Photograph: James Andanson, *Catherine Breillat at Home*, 1975.

Design: Hedi El Kholti
ISBN: 978-1-63590-261-7

10 9 8 7 6 5 4 3 2 1

Distributed by the MIT Press, Cambridge, MA, and London, England
Printed and bound in the United States of America.

I Only Believe in Myself

Conversation with
Murielle Joudet

Translated by
Christine Pichini

semiotext(e)

TABLE OF CONTENTS

AN
OLD
YOUNG
GIRL

Introduction by Murielle Joudet

There are those who write to gain the applause of men by inventing noble sentiments of the heart, which indeed they may even possess. As for me I use my genius to depict the delights of cruelty! No passing joys these, nor are they false, but they were born with Man and will die with him.

—Lautréamont, *Les Chants de Maldoror*

I struggle to allow for the existence of others. In love, particularly, I have a hard time. I only believe in myself. In a romantic relationship, especially a really passionate one, I don't talk. I talk to the person I'm in love with in my head. With my last husband, as soon the car would reach the intersection right before his house, I'd dread getting there. I'd go there hoping for something I wouldn't get, because he didn't know what I wanted. Love makes me outrageous. I argue in my head. I never started anything, never tried anything with a man, even when I was beautiful—they were always the ones who wanted it.

Every morning, I get these "attacks from the abyss." I can't get up because I can't imagine any reason to get up. They usually disappear around eleven o'clock. But if I have something imperative to do, I get up. Cinema is the only imperative left.

—Catherine Breillat, *Abus de faiblesse*

It was summer. Every year, during my vacation from school, I used to spend a very long month visiting my family in Lebanon. Thundering boredom that I looked forward to with increasing anxiety: I crammed my suitcase with books, anticipating those endless nights of insomnia spent under the fan, in decimating humidity, the wall studded with small somber stains made by the corpses of crushed mosquitoes. A large school notebook served as *journal intime*. Once my mother found it, and at the time I thought the damage was irreparable, our relationship would never recover. Entire days spent in a large country club swimming pool, squirming with shame in my bathing suit. After you've been in the chlorinated water a while, you stop swimming, you stay close to the edge and daydream about your life. I remember how the pool handrail surreptitiously transformed into a man. I secretly embraced him, I talked to him, he was my first love.

Night and day, far too much time to think, purulent streams of cerebration leading nowhere, that moment when thought tips irremediably over into angst. Raw, without a net, terrorized by what it discovers. Every day, the desperate waiting for life to finally begin. Freedom—that is to say, adult life, sexual and free—never seemed as far away and impossible to me as it did between July and August.

Catherine Breillat has said it over and over again: summer vacations sharpen the definition of a young girl. I never expected to find all those silent, incommunicable experiences in cinema. I never expected that cinema would represent me, although I had never suffered from the lack of finding myself there: without having even imagined it, I saw myself in a film absolutely. *A Real Young Girl* (*Une vraie jeune fille*), *Fat Girl* (*À ma soeur!*): the invisible Prince Charming in the swimming pool, the auscultation and disgust of one's own body, carceral vacations, being locked inside yourself, miles away from a summer romance. *36 fillette*: disgust as desire's keystone, that demented passivity that organizes a love life, men on the prowl. All the young girls who experience everything too young, and the ones who don't experience any of it, are Catherine Breillat's characters. I think that she's the first to have said that the bildungsroman of adolescence is boredom. She forges herself in the fire of her impatience to start living; because life is slow to start and quick to disappoint us, we accelerate mentally, we dream of disasters, bloodbaths. The young girl is sick of Logos, sick of having to draw a lesson from all her experiences, exhausted by her brain at war with her sex. Above all, the young girl is not mawkish, she's a knife stuck in reality.

My first encounter with Breillat's cinema was, in fact, when I was on summer vacation. In Lebanon, our antiquated television set picked up some international channels: music videos on a loop on MTV, debates on TV5Monde, American films subtitled in Arabic, the beginnings of reality TV—boredom consumed it all. It was still the blessed, and soon extinct, era of films for television made by auteurs. One of them was on again very late, at the stroke of 2 a.m. I caught the story on the fly. Even when you know nothing about cinema, a shot, a real one, the right actors, the perfect line will seek you out wherever you are and refuse to let go. It was *Brief Crossing* (*Brève traversée*), the story of a love affair between a British redhead and a young man that lasts the length of a ferry ride. Aware of the impossibility of their affair surviving outside of that environment, the woman decides not to wait for her secret lover and disappears, leaving an immense void that I still remember vividly—they had confided in each other completely and would never see each other again. In a single journey, the woman gives the boy a sentimental education: Here, take it, your first heartbreak. After all, that's what you wanted.

* * *

I met Catherine Breillat for the first time in 2015. She had agreed to an extended, filmed interview that gave me the opportunity to view her entire oeuvre. Even when her heroines are women over thirty, time still does not blunt the fundamental givens of the young girl, that conceptual character and abstract limit. Even when Breillat films Isabelle Huppert or Léa Drucker, she captures absolute adolescence. In *Romance*, that film that says it all, mercilessly, Caroline Ducey travels through "that paradise of violence and that hell of purity" (Pasolini), after which nothing awaits her but an image, the clearest possible image, of herself. I don't think I have ever seen—again, without seeking it out—such an accurate image of myself.

Until now, we have seen, we have believed, that in passion and sex, the workings of the mind are under pleasure's influence. Breillat says the opposite: When we're in love, the mind becomes inexhaustible, autointoxicated. The brain wrecks everything, all the time, even the very possibility of experiencing something, of experiencing men. We're constantly crashing against the walls of the skull, everywhere, all the time. And the only passion there is to experience only happens with oneself. By obsessively articulating our fundamental curse, that rupture in ourselves (a division between sex and brain, mother and whore, body and mind, stain and purity), Breillat's cinema helped glue us back together, reveal us completely. Showed us that in fact, it all works together: one's brain is in one's sex, one's sex is in one's brain—that was clear.

I remember that before the interview began, while she was getting her makeup done, I wasn't able to start a conversation with her, to grab her attention. Then I realized the extent to which the social lubricant of chitchat was absolutely foreign to her logic. But as soon as the interview began, she transformed, literally lit up. It's worth mentioning here—because it has so much to do with her cinema, with that ontological rupture—the fascinating contrast between her slowed-down movements, hampered by her stroke, and the fury of her thinking. If her body makes you think the opposite, you very quickly learn: Catherine Breillat is always going faster than you, drowning you in her intransigence. Even if you have prepared for weeks on end, searching for the thing that's never been said about her cinema, she'll snuff out all of your intellectual pretensions. Her body has become one of the many traps that have been set by her intelligence.

She had turned me around, before she disappeared into a taxi, leaving me thrilled and exhausted on the curb. From that moment on, a gnawing desire to recreate that moment rose in me, coupled with the sense of a kind of responsibility: I had to try to circumnavigate that brain, file everything this woman knows in a book—it would be useful, someone might come across the book by chance, decades later, in a library, and be saved by it. Plus, above and beyond the themes that anyone could recognize, her greatness as a filmmaker must be reiterated, and her method documented: from writing to editing, from her obsession with painters and writers who "extend their hand to her through the centuries," to her tempestuous passion for her actors.

I have occasionally retained certain answers and remarks which, while they might seem parasitic, dispensable, and not worthy of the "final cut," seemed to me to compose a more accurate, cumulative portrait of Catherine Breillat—and of our relationship. It seemed to me that by not overly cleansing the text of its dross, I was able to render a more accurate image of what an interview is: a space that is not only ethereal, purely intellectual, but shot through with randomness, fatigue, repetitions, questions that fall by the wayside, digressions, and excessive expressions. To attempt to smooth out these rough edges would be to distort and diminish the character.

* * *

This book is the fruit of thirty hours of interviews that took place between September 2022 and March 2023, followed by long edits made via telephone. Our meetings always took place on Saturdays, around 2 p.m. At the time, she was staying in a borrowed apartment in Saint-Germain-de-Prés, and in the middle of editing *Last Summer* (*L'été dernier*). In that large, empty, very quiet apartment, a few objects caught my eye and became, in my memory, inseparable from this book: a red brass teapot (which appears in her most recent film), an enormous bottle of Guerlain perfume, and butter, which was always outside of the fridge and which I would systematically put away.

The flow of our conversation prevented us from noticing that night was gradually falling in the apartment. I'd emerge after three hours, always exhausted, wondering what would happen if I waited for her to tire before me—we'd probably be up all night. When you're near her, you get the impression that her ideas, her vision of things, reign over the world—that there are no others. The first time I left her apartment, I came across an old Livre de Poche edition of *Une vieille maîtresse* sitting there in the street. Proof that the world had suddenly turned Breillatian. This anecdote is of a pair with another that summarizes the matter: Breillat spends part of the year on the island of Bréhat.

I had this same feeling of entering into another temporality two other times in my life, with Jean-Claude Brisseau and Philippe Garrel. Three absolutely obsessional filmmakers whom you approach as if you were approaching a bonfire. The things that don't exist in their eyes (social networks, other people's cinema, television, emails, whatever) don't exist, period. In their orbit, they make their ideas prevail, without exerting any kind of authority. Simply by their way of being concentrated on themselves, of talking only about the three or four things that matter in their lives, their cinema. It's an intransigence that reframes you, sets you straight. You leave thinking that you have to live by these obsessions, and not by other things. You have to sort through it, clear the decks.

It seemed as if she hadn't moved from one week to the next, that she had stayed there, sitting on the sofa, thinking about my questions, ruminating over her answers, always obsessed with reclarifying her thinking to be as clear as possible—to sharpen her phrases as if they were knives. One afternoon, I saw her from far away, coming back from shopping (exactly like the shot of Huppert in *Abuse of Weakness* [*Abus de faiblesse*]). In the elevator, she immediately picked up the thread of the last comment I had made three weeks earlier: "I'm not a mother, I'm an auteur!" She remembered the sentence we had ended on precisely. It seemed totally inconceivable to me that she had eaten, slept, lived in the interval between the two interviews.

At first, I was studious, carefully preparing my questions, following a chronological order, beginning with provincial life and *A Real Young Girl*. But she had decided otherwise: it was impossible to divert her from a long anecdote about *36 fillette*. During our second meeting, I understood the lesson: less preparation, more listening. I slipped into the folds of a monologue which I vaguely attempted to inflect and which I got in the way of more than anything else. Sometimes I arrived determined, less tired, reminding myself that it was my book (it wasn't my book at all, in fact), asking questions three or four times until I got an answer. I tried everything to regain control, to enter the citadel, but a filmmaker willing to do anything to obtain the image she wants will also be willing to do anything to pursue her thinking.

Despite the fatigue, a sort of addiction to her intelligence took root: I wanted to explore her mind, wanted her to tell me what she thought about the slightest thing, the most minor film. I returned to the Rue des Beaux-Arts as soon as I could, resumed our meeting so I could catch a few final, sublime sentences, her "punchlines" that came from wherever, whenever—the most important thing to remember was to turn off the tape recorder only at the very last minute, once the door was closed, not before. She had become the Dragon, and I was a valiant knight off to rescue I don't know what—the book, maybe—from her clutches.

I arrived with the arrogance of the critic who expected to reveal things to Breillat that she hadn't seen, hadn't intellectualized, and I ran into the wall of her monstrous intellect. She was the one who showed me things, the one who told me what her oeuvre was about, along with everything else: men, women, sexuality, actors, a woman's life. I was the one who left knowing more. I understood that she wasn't a wise, old woman at all, but still and always a young girl. She's still making films to disobey her mother, the world, to defy the unfilmable, that magnificent word that repeatedly comes out of her mouth. Plus, and I'll say it here because I'm afraid that it may not become clear in what follows, I carry with me another of her lessons: you must have enough pride to withstand everything, the supreme elegance never to complain, although, as she told me over the telephone, "life makes you the victim of plenty of things, those are the rules."

Everything in her memory exists in the present; time has caused nothing to recede into the background. She tells you a forty-year-old anecdote as if she were a teenager, proud of her latest folly; she remembers a boy from her adolescence as if she had spurned him the night before. When I think about her, I still wonder, every day, how she does it, being herself, dragging her awareness over things without exhausting herself or, conversely, boring herself to death. She is an impossible woman, an old young girl who has this crazy, improbable habit of never adapting to her interlocutor: she only has one version of herself in reserve. That seems to me to be a satisfying definition of what it means to be an artist.

The things that she says can be heard nowhere else, she's the only one who can say them—and so we had to go back, again and again. Her absolutely unique mind doesn't encourage you to think like her but to stylize your own thinking, to protect it from the assaults of conformism, of laziness—thinking like other people in order to be at ease with your era. On the red carpet of the last Festival de Cannes, she arrived transformed, stunning, decked out as a platinum blonde à la Jean Harlow, her heavy black boot that was cleverly revealed through the slit in her virginal Dior gown, holding the metallic handle of her ebony cane—the look of an S-M queen—all of it meant to say that one must have style in everything in life. It's the only way to make it livable.

And then, and I don't mean this in a negative way, when Catherine Breillat looks at you, it's her own reflection that she sees. It's a very peculiar thing, but I don't think that she's emerged from her inner journey, from her first open *journal intime*. She's remained there, as if imprisoned, and looks at you through the filter of that journal that's always in progress. You can never fully explore such a sensibility—you leave frustrated, saving from oblivion little fragments of Breillat's infinite conversation with herself, which began as soon as her consciousness allowed it, and which will continue without you.

At the end of our first interview, night had fallen over the apartment, and we hadn't felt the impulse to turn on a lamp. She wanted to show me some images of her young actor, Samuel Kircher, that she was searching for on her computer. The halo of the screen dimly illuminated her face. She was in such a state of rapture that I realized that all of real life—things to do, meetings, meals, friends—was only an obstacle, an annoying intermission between herself and that image, and every other image that shines in the night of her cinema. She was so absorbed by her actor that she ended up forgetting I was there, and I left without her noticing.

I DIDN'T WANT TO BE A VIRGIN

The gaze of shame • Viridiana is me • I thought that nightclubs were the most important thing in the world • a seducer of Lolitas, a tainted Casanova • there's always something unraveling with men • *Baby Doll* • like seagulls • you have to be a masochist to love men • *36 fillette* • Rhett Butler and all of literature's chauvinists • *L'homme facile* • I organized with myself • we have all been raped • I am not scandalous, I am a scandal • basically, I only like adolescents • I'm well aware that I'm Maldoror • *Mary Magdalene in Ecstasy* • Mona Lisa's smile, but with the eyelid • done, like a slab of meat

Catherine Breillat: My mother was humiliated by having two daughters, especially the second. And plus, she said I was butt-ugly, bald, with bulges instead of eyebrows. I looked like Taras Bulba.[1] Bringing home this second daughter was a humiliation. In her eyes, men were the only good thing. I don't blame my mother, not at all. At the time, there was a kind of shame in being a woman, in having female genitalia.[2] You had to pretend it didn't exist; you couldn't have any dignity if you had a female sex. None. That's why I detest, absolutely detest Freud: I never felt I had a missing penis. I thought what boys had was excessive: something visible, something that swung back and forth, that was much worse. I wondered how they could stand having that between their legs. I pitied them. I never had a missing penis. I did, however, have missing rights.

Murielle Joudet: *How did your mother make you experience that shame?*

She taught me what they call modesty [*pudeur*]: shame of oneself, denial. She taught me to be so ashamed of my own body that I developed the greatest contempt for her. Because she brought me into the world, she must have spread her legs, the gynecologist must have removed the baby ... You had to deny that you had a sex, keep it absolutely secret, because if anyone knew, you'd be despised, and considered obscene. That's the foundation of my cinema. It's fundamental, and it comes from somewhere very far away. That contempt was incompatible with the enormous pride that I have. Adults created a world where I wasn't there, where I didn't have the right to exist. And

---

1. Eponymous character of Nikolai Gogol's novel (1843).
2. Breillat was born in 1948.

yet I never wanted to be anything other than myself. I directed *Romance* and *Anatomy of Hell* (*Anatomie de l'enfer*) to prove that nothing is ever obscene.

Were you seeking to remedy that shame with your oeuvre, or had you already rid yourself of it beforehand?

Not at all, that shame has always been there. I remember a lunch I had with Roberto Rossellini very clearly, it was the night before I began shooting *A Real Young Girl* (*Une vraie jeune fille*). I was twenty-two years old—check that, I'm always wrong about dates—and I already knew I was a great director. I must have been horribly arrogant, a little annoying, and he asked me, "What do you think you're going to add to the portrayal of young girls that hasn't already been done by men?" I can still see the restaurant and the way I answered him without missing a beat: "The gaze of shame. Because you're the ones who gave us our shame, and we're the ones who carry it."

Who believed in you?

No one, just me! At the Ciné-club in Niort, I saw my first film in a theatre: Bergman's *Sawdust and Tinsel* (1953). It was a shock; I recognized myself for the first time. My fictional body was there in Harriet Andersson, and what she did in that film went against everything that I was taught about what a young girl should be. That film was me. Actually, no, not yet. The second film I saw was Buñuel's *Viridiana* (1961): when I think about it, I can't help it, I don't see the actress Silvia Pinal's face, only my own. *Stardust and Tinsel* is my fictional body, the body of my characters. Viridiana is me.

You wrote your first novel, L'homme facile (Easy man), *when you were seventeen. What story did you want to tell?*

I wrote *Le Libanais* (*The Lebanese*) first: I had no subject, I hadn't experienced anything yet, so I told the story of the rape attempt I survived when I was fourteen—the novel was never published but it inspired *36 fillette*. At the time, I thought that nightclubs were the most important thing in the world. A night that wasn't spent in a club was a wasted night. We spent our vacations in Bayonne. My great-aunt lent us her villa on the Allées Paulmy. Every night, my sister and I waited until our parents were asleep to crawl out the window. Two young fourteen- and fifteen-year-old girls hitchhiking in the middle of the night to go to a club in Biarritz; it was nuts. Strangely enough, they let us in, I realized a posteriori that they thought we were young taxi dancers.

What happened in that nightclub?

I met a guy who was supposedly a Spanish grandee, who licensed Pepsi-Cola. He lived in the Hôtel du Palais during the holidays—his wealth was the perfect showcase for his beauty. He had a white convertible Thunderbird with blood-red leather seats, and he looked like José Luis de Vilallonga, a very chic Spanish actor. He was the first man to pique my interest, but it wasn't at all sexual, instead it was a kind of recognition of elegance and charm, the kind you find with João César Monteiro when he's acting. A seducer of arrogant Lolitas, a tainted charmer. He always invited me to his table where I could drink free Pepsis, and he asked me to slow dance. But as soon as I got attached to him, he stopped being an image, I could only see one thing: his age. I saw the slightly aging skin, I saw all the wrinkles that, from a distance, were imperceptible—I always see that in my actors, I'm terrible. I felt a kind of disgust for this person, who was definitely very seductive, but who was already decaying—he was moving toward death. I actually have gay tastes: I don't like men, I only like boys. Before their age gives them that masculine false superiority. There's always something unraveling with men, at least from the perspective of a young girl of fourteen, which is, deep down, always my perspective. That guy seduced me, and at the same time, I found him repulsive.

Something about that is fundamental to your cinema: the disgust that structures female sexuality. Why is it so important? Why, with women, can disgust be the driving force behind desire?

Oh, yeah, that too! Again, I come back to my own story, because adolescence is a muddle, and you sort it out afterward … One night, I had a date with that guy and I was waiting in a café near the casino in Biarritz when I saw Serge Golovine coming out, he was a great dancer-choreographer who, like Rudolf Nureyev, began his career very late. He was surrounded by women in formal gowns who were asking for his autograph. He saw me waiting, arrogant and uptight, and asked if I wanted one—such a humiliating thing. I answered without skipping a beat: "No, I definitely don't want an autograph!" I just wanted to talk to someone like me, I wanted to know if his parents had made fun of him when he was my age, and if he had been confident that he would become a great dancer and star. My parents made fun of me. And I realize that meeting with Serge Golovine was a formative experience for me. He spent hours in the freezing cold talking with me. In *36 fillette*, Jean-Pierre Léaud plays him, I made him a pianist named Boris Golovine—I was incapable of changing anything other than his first name ... When I went back to the nightclub at almost two in the morning, my Spanish grandee was on edge, he had been waiting for me for hours. Even though I was still glowing from my meeting with Golovine, I had a terrible headache. He suggested we go find some aspirin in his hotel room, so, like a goose, I followed him with complete confidence.

So there's Golovine, the artist who speaks to your mind, to your vocation, and then there's the dandy waiting for you in the club who is after your body. You had no idea?

No! Despite what you see in *36 fillette*. The truth is he immediately threw me down on the floor saying that I had a woman's body (my chest measured thirty-six inches), that I looked like a woman and so I should "take it like a woman." I was wearing sailor's pants that I had bought mail-order from *ELLE* magazine. They had buttons all over them, and it was impossible to figure out how to take them off. We fought for three hours, he never managed to get them off me. Once he had been worn down, he pulled his cock out and must have asked me for a hand job or a blow job, I don't remember. I couldn't possibly have understood, either way. At that time I didn't even know that men got hard. The only image I had of a man's sex was from little boys or babies. On the other hand, I knew what you had to do to defend yourself against a man. I grabbed his balls and squeezed them with all the strength I had. He started screaming, screaming, screaming ... and I wouldn't loosen my grip. He tried to strangle me to get me to let go—there are strangulations in all of my films, I don't know if you've noticed … I let go of him, he let go of me, he yelled at me because he had almost killed me. He was in a state of shock. Everything in the bedroom was broken. Then, with a kind of sovereign pride, I picked myself up, told him he was a pig and that I needed to wash up. I treated him with total contempt, giving him orders—like in the film. And still, when I went and stood naked in the bathroom before I took a shower, I carefully left the door open. That's where it starts looking like the film.

That's what you see in 36 fillette: *Lili (Delphine Zentout) circulates in a zone of undecidability. She seems not to know what she wants, or what she doesn't want.*

It's strange, you can have the feeling both of having been raped and of having wanted it a little. I should have subtitled the film "or, How Young Girls Ask for Their Own Rape." Because desire is forbidden, because you're not allowed to have it, you have to transfer the culpability to a man. He has to be the guilty one.

Regarding the question of rape, you are part of a lineage of feminists who try to defend the idea that you can recover from rape, that you don't have to feel traumatized.

Although rape is a crime that is in itself traumatizing, and that is difficult to recover from, it's society that forces victims to feel as if their lives have been ruined. The rapist is a criminal, yes, but rape in itself doesn't change you. What changes you is the ruthless injunction ordering a victim to behave as an emblematic victim. We have to be able to dissociate the fact that while for me, the victim, it's better to get up and consider it as nothing, for the rapist it's still a crime—that's a fundamental distinction. If it means nothing to me, it's because I've managed to pull myself out of the feminine condition that I've been stuffed into like a sack, like when they drown stray cats and mice.

In 36 fillette, you open up a space to observe that up close: repulsion, disgust, the desire to go there, flirting …

If we really examine it, sometimes we don't even know what we wanted. Let's just say that it's complicated and all of my cinema is built from that complicated thing. I wrote an article in *Le Monde* where I explained that there wasn't any difference between flirting and sleeping together and I always find that from a moral point of view, there isn't any difference at all. What makes us back down from saying yes to a boy is the stupid education we're given that makes us compartmentalize things, this injunction not to sleep together on the first date. Flirting is there to tame your emotions, even if you don't have to do anything. I find foreplay delicious, how you pretend that you don't know if you're going to sleep together, even though it's obvious. Then, little by little, you get used to the idea because you can't do without each other anymore. It's like birds: Seagulls spend three years becoming a couple. Every year, they meet and learn to speak together, to tune their voices, that's how they recognize each other. And the second year, they learn more, and the third year, they actually mate for life. That's what flirting is all about. It means you get used to each other until it becomes ultra necessary, you call each other ten times a day, you kiss constantly. In married life, kissing becomes much more rare. Flirting is champagne fizz.

With this issue of structural disgust, isn't it deep down the idea that we are fundamentally masochistic?

I've explained it to feminists who ultimately got it. They were horrified by the masochistic things in my films. I told them that feminism can't exist if you don't take into account the fact that women have sons, are mothers, love men. To be able to love them, you have to be masochistic, it's a necessity, otherwise you hate them—even if I'm only masochistic for my own pleasure, never the other's. But yes, men are hateful because of the way in which they've treated us for centuries and the way that they look at us. You have to be a masochist to love them; it can't be any other way, and so we have to analyze that.

This business of desire born from disgust is exactly the story of Baby Doll *(Elia Kazan, 1956), a film that you often reference.*

After *Nocturnal Uproar* (*Tapage nocturne*), my second film, I didn't want to make films anymore, I couldn't come up with any ideas and I especially didn't want to be stoned to death again. I wanted to go live on my own private island and be a writer, since it wasn't worth it to be a director anymore. Then I went to see Elia Kazan's *Baby Doll* at the Christine Cinéma Club, where they were playing it on a loop—I stayed from noon until midnight. Directors save me, painters too. They extend their hand to me across the centuries, that's the way it is. The day after that, I started writing *36 fillette*: I wove *Baby Doll* into that story of the attempted rape I experienced at fourteen. That's my definition of a great film: as soon as I leave the theatre, I want to create cinema. I am Baby Doll: I am Carroll Baker, but also Eli Wallach. *Baby Doll* is *Beauty and the Beast*, a story I've always loved: the young girl falls in love with the man who shames her. Eli Wallach is sublime because he's everything you detest and everything that attracts you, he's brutal, sexy, intelligent. And at the same time, you're ashamed, like I could feel ashamed of Toscan.[3] In fact, I called him Rogozhin, then the Bourgeois Gentleman. I couldn't handle being affectionate with him in public. It was exactly like *Baby Doll*, in the end.

That's all you talk about, disgust and shame.

About Rhett Butler and all of literature's chauvinists. The attraction to the person who covets you and will inevitably humiliate you.

Male filmmakers perhaps don't think as much about masculine identity, whereas women filmmakers are eventually ordered to think about their identity.

They don't think about anything at all. They exist in the denial of the laws they concoct against us to keep us under their control. They define themselves according to a tutelary principle and we have to be these very pretty and fragile women they have the ancestral duty to protect—yes, to oppress! They don't know women. While we, we don't have any choice, we're so locked into "Shut up and look pretty" that we're forced to redo everything, to retrace our steps. I practice "Know thyself" in all of my films. I'm not ashamed to show every kind of depravity, I'm familiar with it. I don't glory in it, but I know that it exists: you can love something

3. Daniel Toscan du Plantier (1941–2003), film producer.
4. The hero of Margaret Mitchell's *Gone with the Wind* (1936).

that you're ashamed of, things you don't really want to shout from the rooftops. Because that's what life is, that's what it means to live and to have an awareness of it. Otherwise, you die without even having encountered yourself.

In your films, the question of sexuality overlaps with the question of fear: sexuality is anxiety producing. You're afraid of getting pregnant, afraid of being a whore. Is it anxiety that you're filming?

Of course, because virginity is a loss, you lose value. Lili says it when her father hits her and asks her if she has slept with Maurice. Her reply sounds like a scathing reproach addressed to her father and mother: "I can't sleep with Maurice, I can't sleep with him, I just can't!" Because of them, it becomes too hard for her to abandon herself. That's the fundamental mutilation. No longer simply abandoning yourself to what you want to do.

It's too hard to regress to an animal level, to put the mind aside.

Although I'm mentally straight as an arrow, my relationship with my body is bad because it got screwed up for me, and even my relationships with men and with the world. I constructed myself against, against, against. I was a very happy, very boisterous little girl, and all of that was taken away from me. My mother was incredibly suspicious because I had already matured at twelve; it was shameful. Everything became shameful. The fact that I didn't know anything. It's not hard to be a woman, it's *unique* because you have to fight against the entire world to say: I'm pure, I exist, I am, not less than other people but at least as much, if not more.

I think it must have been very complicated for you to join a feminist movement, to organize with other women.

I organized with myself. I'm not collective at all; I can't be because in order to defend yourself, you need a unique mindset that you have to create on your own. That didn't prevent me from being feminist; I've always been one. It was essential for me to be, otherwise I would have hated myself.

The female body is a body that doesn't belong to itself. In your films, you specifically try to belong to yourself, to restore yourself to yourself, body and soul.

Women's bodies belong to virginity, which society keeps an exact account of—that's the story told in *A Real Young Girl* and *Fat Girl* (*À ma soeur!*). The virginity of girls belongs to society. That's the social and primordial violation. We have all been raped. I didn't want to be a virgin, I wanted my father to get me an operation, so that no man could have me as a virgin. It's a sort of nauseating thing, that membrane that's located who knows where ... I still don't know where and I don't want to know. It disgusts me and repulses me and that repulsion belongs to society. But anyway, I want to keep going with the rape story because beginnings are always a muddle ...

So I forced the Spanish grandee to take me to find my sister; of course that idiot was still hanging out with no idea what time it was, even though we had to get back home before our parents discovered we were gone. I was covered in bruises, I have no idea how my parents didn't notice. I wasn't seriously injured, sexually or mentally, but still, it was super violent. And I wasn't going to press charges: I was fourteen years old and I had snuck out.

But I decided that I should use it for something. I should use it to become a writer. Every cloud has a silver lining: my whole life obeys that rule. Disasters, heartaches, strokes, all of it must be used to create an oeuvre, everything must be sublimated. And so I launched into writing my first book, *Le Libanais*, I had it bound and page numbered. A totally childish book about that rape that ultimately didn't succeed but was still an absolute debasement, and that ultimately did succeed in creating a literary awakening.

That means that your oeuvre finds its origin in sexual violence; it's the primal scene. In Abuse of Weakness *(Abus de faiblesse)*, *it's the same thing: people said that you got into that relationship with Christophe Rocancourt because you could see the great story it would make. To what extent do you experience things because there's a film at the end?*

With Rocancourt, I was in a state ... I was in total denial of how serious my stroke was. I had decided to never complain, and the film projects I had were terrifying. I had to do impossible things, even though I had become human debris ... But *Abuse of Weakness*, I have trouble talking about it because I still don't understand it. I thought I was past crying every time I talked about it.

Should we decide not to talk about it?

We'll talk about it but not right away; I think it's crucial that we talk about it, actually. That's where the psychological flaw is, and I haven't come to understand what happened. I was disabled, drugged, you can see how I walk. I had to be in denial in order to live. But to go back to my story ...

So I do this novel, *Le Libanais*, with this violet cover that was totally Vasarely, and I send the book to the editor Jean-Jacques Pauvert. His reader had handed him a blank page with the words "Disconcerting, but garbage" written on it in chicken scratches. Pauvert, intrigued by that unusually pithy assassination, read the manuscript and asked to see me. In the state it was in, frankly the book was totally unpublishable, it was the book of a fourteen-year-old who only cared about nightclubs. It was stupid, but there was still something worth saving from all that infantileness, it was very *Almanach Vermot*. Pauvert asked me to rework it. But how do you rework a manuscript that's already been bound? That was an impasse for me. Straight away I wrote another book: *L'homme facile*, which was my first real book. I reread it recently and it's too bad that Christian Bourgois, who edited it, didn't make me rework it more. I wrote it in the man's voice, in the first person, it's actually really crazy. Then I moved to the third person. I may be the third person, I always keep a certain distance from myself, the distance of fiction. The book was banned for anyone under eighteen, although I was seventeen. That meant that when it was written, I wasn't allowed to reread myself—I was forbidden from myself. I love that phrase. It's ironic, but also a fundamental wound. I am not scandalous, I am a scandal. It was a scandal to be what I was at seventeen. Society couldn't tolerate me without dressing me up with shocking or scandalous adjectives.

The fixation of your oeuvre is really the young girl, you never say "woman." Let's just say that you haven't followed your body's own development.

I loathe the assignment. Becoming, being a woman. I'd rather stay mentally stuck at fourteen! Not having matured, and having the same enthusiasm about literature and films that I love, the enthusiasm of a baby, or a fanatical teenager. Basically, I only like adolescents, when anything's possible in life, when you dream, when you get enthusiastic. When I read Lautréamont, it's like a spiritual epic: everything is possible, transparent, magic. I'm well aware that I'm Maldoror. When you're young, everything you want to do, you do. And at the time, I wanted to make a film but I didn't know how to go about it. Because of people like Robbe-Grillet and Romain Gary, I was persuaded that if I wrote a book, someone would ask to adapt it for the cinema.

What are some things you can't stand seeing in a film?

I detest compunction, the brakes people put on speaking the truth. I like the violence of thought, the violence of the truth, of words. Political correctness, "feminist" correctness, doesn't bother me. But feminism is about rights, it isn't literature or cinema. The films that feel obligated to tell a story that's already in the newspapers—why tell it again? Cinema is an art, not a political tool, even if there are great political films. But the opportunistic machine of the moment that we see everywhere, that annoys me. I was just making a list of great films for Samuel Kircher.[5] I only put geniuses on it. I only watch their films, the others bore me.

Are there any recent films that you've liked?

Recently I haven't seen anything, because I have to say, I can't get around, I can't walk at night anymore. I can't see a thing,

---

3. Actor in *Last Summer*, the film that Breillat was editing at the time of the interview.

everything is too unstable and I have no balance. I don't know where the left side of my body is, I have to see it. Unfortunately, I've never stood up straight, because as soon as I had breasts, I had complexes about it and started hunching over. So I don't stand up straight, which is very bad for a hemiplegic who has to stand up very straight to maintain her balance.

But you can watch films at home. I'd like to know what interests you.

What interests me is watching a masterpiece fifty times, more than watching something light once. I can't stand distraction. I always say that distracting yourself is always avoiding something. I'm terribly serious.

You're not curious about what's being made?

Not at all. When I see how it's filmed, the lines, actors I don't like …

Bruno Dumont, you're interested in him, right?

I like him, Bruno Dumont, we think very highly of each other. Now, a film like *Camille Claudel 1915* (2013), I liked that so much I was jealous. The film came out at the same time as *Abuse of Weakness*. I told him, "It's really annoying, your film is better than mine!" It's absolutely, dizzyingly great. Although at the beginning I was wondering, "Why is he making a *biopic* about Camille Claudel?" But I was blown away. You have to blow me away, otherwise I'm not interested. I've been a juror in festivals many times: your eyes get weighed down by the mediocrity.

So your eyes shouldn't get weighed down, it could be dangerous?

No, it's not that it's dangerous; let's just say that watching essential things transports you, makes you want to do something, and that creates you. The unessential things, that's about re-creation, that doesn't *create* you. That doesn't take you outside of yourself to finally become great, especially when you're as infirm and slumped over as I am.

You seem different on a shoot, you come out of yourself.

Yes, completely, I'm another person. I'm much too shy to do what I do, so you better believe that I become someone else. To my great astonishment, I no longer hide behind a scarf when I'm watching the monitor, so I must have changed.

Why did you do that, incidentally?

It's the only way for me to concentrate without people seeing how concentrated and delighted I am. I hide the fascination I feel when I'm filming and observing my actors. Otherwise, I'd have to mask my facial expressions and fall short of my job as a director.

And how do you know what you want?

I only see it on the monitor. I can see that the actor only needs to tilt her head back a little, and that's it, there's the image. On *Last Summer* (*L'été dernier*), I was tormented by the idea of filming Léa Drucker having an orgasm in close-up, I thought that it would be too crude an image, that it would make her look old and ugly, I couldn't envision it. How do you sculpt that? How do you shape what she carves out from within to discover truth, emotion, ease? A face offered up to the camera that breathes, that has emotions, possibly even exaltation. It's incredible when that happens. I didn't want her to look ugly. And I thought of Caravaggio's *Mary Magdalene in Ecstasy*, which I looked at all night on the internet; actually, you can't tell if she is in ecstasy or if she's dying. To my great astonishment, I thought that she was a young girl, but she isn't at all: she has exactly the same nostrils as Léa. It's Léa, and she is infinitely beautiful. So we had to tilt her head backward, her neck in that unbelievable arch ... That's perfection, not a single wrinkle, just the pictorial magic of Caravaggio. When you do a love scene, you have to always place the body and the head on a diagonal, that's what painters do, it's a rule. Painters have studied poses and frames their entire lives, it's not worth reinventing the wheel, everything they do applies perfectly to cinema.

What kind of painting matters the most to you?

The sixteenth and seventeenth centuries. I adore Raphael. Actually, I love them all: Titian, Botticelli. I borrowed their soul, since the soul is what counts. I have this thing about the eyelid that comes from quattrocento. That kind of transparency, it's like Mona Lisa's smile, but with the eyelid. There is very little flesh in those paintings, but what flesh there is is incandescent. It's sublime because it's sublimated. It's a very particular type of light that materializes like a screen, and the face has to spread out over the screen, which creates a kind of vertigo. Painters position the irises of the eyes in a certain way, and that's not something the actors can know. I'm the one who has to say, "No, cast your eye downward." That detail changes the entire meaning of the scene. Painting, after all, has a kind of *écriture* that's embedded in our minds. Basically, I consider myself to be a painter.

What are you prepared to do to get the image you want?

When I want an image, I have absolutely no pride, no shame, and no mercy, either. I don't care how grotesque I am, as long as I get it. I devote as much time and energy (and at a certain point, film) as it requires. When I want my image, I'm like a child at play, and everyone can see that. So at some point yes, I became willing to do anything. Pialat told me that for *The Mouth Agape* (1974), he needed a corpse and had his mother disinterred. He used a screwdriver to turn her head so that she could be perfectly in frame. There obviously may be some moral condemnation, but I myself don't condemn anyone who isn't hurting anyone else to get what he wants. In *A Real Young Girl*, when she's crawling across the beach with feathers in her ass saying that she's a chicken, I can't tell you how much blinding shame we had to overcome to film that. Or when she's spread-eagled with the wire with the earthworm on her sex: I gave myself a hell of a time, I had to go to the Basque region to find an earthworm because there weren't any in the sand where we were shooting, in the Landes. I knew we needed a large one to represent a man's sex.

I always wonder: When you're shooting, do you make the scene correspond to an image in your head, or do you look for and find it during shooting?

I find it in the moment. That's what amuses me the most; I have fun playing on a shoot. I've learned that. I'm a creature of the set, I discover everything in the moment. And how could you do it any other way? We're working with human material, after all. Before Saïd found me,[6] I was living in Portugal, not caring about anything, like a piece of meat, doing nothing, waiting for death, I had lost all interest in life. And then I get on set and that's it, I recreate my world, I have fun, so much fun.

---

6. Saïd Ben Saïd, the producer of *Last Summer*.

CATHERINE & CO.

Two reasons why guys leave me • I don't remember having loved my mother • I was made for the simple happiness of fools • I don't have to check off my sex • *A Real Young Girl* • I write things to force myself to film them • my best required friend • I loved to destroy and I loved shattered beauty • she looks at life that way, almost as if she were buried • you make a film alone, you don't have fun • Petit Bateau, that was my dream • a beautiful girl like you • David Hamilton • a school-play version of Shakespeare isn't Shakespeare • I prostituted myself with that script • *Last Tango in Paris* • these new mini-Savonarolas • balls aren't cerebral hemispheres

Murielle Joudet: *In the elevator, you told me, "I'm not a mother, I'm an auteur."*[7] *Why do you oppose those two terms?*

Catherine Breillat: As a young girl, I never wanted to be a mother, but to invent the world that belonged to me: to create cinema, to write. Under no circumstances did I want to be a mother. My mother was a mother and that didn't make me want to be one. I love my children, but that's not my identity at all. When Philippe Bouvard asked me why I said in *ELLE* that I didn't want children even though I had just had one, I answered, "I dislike people so much that I had to make one that I like."

You don't like other people?

They don't like me, so why should I like them?

But you liked your husbands?

Yes, but when I married my first husband, I knew I'd end up divorcing him. I never even took his name.

Did you like taking care of your children?

The birth of Paul, my third child, and the fact that I couldn't bring myself to imagine being separated from him delayed

---

7. It's very important for me not to put the [feminizing] *e* at the end, because my identity is an auteur. I made a list of all those magnificent feminine words that end in *-eur: peur* [fear], *torpeur* [torpor], *frayeur* [fright], *horreur* [horror], *stupeur* [stupor], *pâleur* [pallor], *douleur* [suffering], *noirceur* [darkness], *apesanteur* [weightlessness] … I could quote you fifty. You'd have to be illiterate to want to feminize *auteur* at the cost of massacring the French language."

shooting *Perfect Love* (*Parfait amour!*) for at least two years. As soon as I see them, as soon the faces of my children appear in close-up, it's just like with my actors, I think about them all day. It's a bona fide alienation, I get stupid. When I'm pregnant, I don't like them. But as soon as I see their transparent eyelids, the adoration in their eyes, their trust … I never get bored. I couldn't tear myself away from Paul. Making the film was impossible. I love them madly, my kids, you mustn't think that I'm a bad mother. But the fact remains that I'm built for cinema, otherwise I'm not built at all. Otherwise, I'm just a heap of laziness.

Did your husbands take care of the children?

Not at all. And besides, kids separate couples. I was right. Because love is romantic, and then all of a sudden you've got diapers, the fridge, the babysitter, getting up early in the morning … Everything becomes prosaic. Children and making a film, two reasons why guys leave me. It's only recently that men have started taking care of the kids; my sons take care of theirs a lot. My kids never blame their father, they blame me for not having done everything right because I was making films and telling stories drawn from real life. For that, they really blame me.

What do they think of your films?

They only liked the last one. My daughter Salomé was totally scarred because at school, they said, "Your mom makes porno films." And then when I left to make my films, my mother was the one who took care of them. But she hated girls, so she was very nice with Hadrien and as atrocious with Salomé as she had been with me. I don't remember—but that must be wrong, like how I see myself in *Viridiana*—nevertheless, I don't remember having loved my mother. It's strange, though, because that can't possibly be true. On the other hand, I remember that I would have been a very normal young girl if they hadn't wanted to diminish me. I was made for the simple happiness of fools. It's life that made me slip, like on an old banana peel that someone forgot to throw in the garbage. All those rotten clichés, that education that's made to stunt you rather than raise you.

I have the impression that motherhood is not a part of your fictional world.

My daughter really blames me. With my children, whom I totally adored, I've realized that I wasn't such a good mother. It's not enough to love them, that's too easy, and I think I'm completely selfish. I gave them tons of presents, all the things that I couldn't even buy myself. I'm an erratic artist whose income is sometimes atrociously scarce, so I never know when it will ever come around again. My life is really a tightrope. But I think I didn't talk to them enough. I didn't have any real communication with them, once they became adolescents. I'm still blown away by my own adolescence, that's the only thing I understand.

Let's go back to your youth in Paris. What was Paris like when you landed there in the '60s? Did you know what you wanted to do? And your sister ...

Followed me. She followed me to Paris, otherwise she would have gone to law school in Bordeaux. I told my parents that I wanted to go to an oriental-language school that only existed in Paris. Once we were there, my sister and I lived on very little money, we only ate bread, brioches, and croissants, and spent all of our nights at Bus Palladium. I slept every night with whomever, I'd modestly undress and wrap myself up in a towel, just like Jane Birkin in *Catherine & Co.*[8] Even with the men I liked, there's no way I would have ever done anything with them, for the simple reason that I had to sleep in their bed. Touching me was out of the question. Sleeping is sleeping: uttering that mantra before I crawled into their bed seemed to me to be warning enough. Sometimes, I spent half the night talking their ears off, fending them off with my elbow—like in my films—until they let me sleep. No one dared go beyond that.

You act in a TV movie by Jean-Roger Cadet (Madame Quinze, 1969) in which a man asks you to smile, and you do it. It's pretty fascinating to think that you could have ended up that way: you could have become an actress, because at that time, it was the only thing that women were allowed to do.

I almost played Yvonne de Galais in *The Wanderer* (Jean-Gabriel Albicocco, 1967). Luckily, they didn't pick me, because deep down I only want to be a director. I want to watch, I want my gaze to seize, to swallow people. I made *A Real Young Girl* because of François, my first husband. Ultimately he's the only one who really loved me: he locked me up in a room so I could write. Like Cocteau locked up Raymond Radiguet. François is the one who found the money for me to make my first film. Otherwise, men hate it when you become an auteur.

8. Film by Michel Boisrond, with a screenplay by Breillat (1975).

A Real Young Girl, which you shot in 1975, has something wild about it, as if it were a page torn not only from cinema but also from France itself.

That's exactly how it was described, wild and unauthorized, because we didn't ask the CNC, or anyone else, for anything. We set out with tons of '60s clothes, endless pairs of stilettos that I bought for a hundred francs, Deruelle makeup, and a 35 mm camera. On the way, we even picked up the carcass of a beautiful white Labrador that we used in the beach scenes. Since I didn't know anything, and was inspired by American hyperrealistic painters, the camerawork is very frontal. In principle, that's never done, but I didn't have principles. I wanted to make a film that was on the edge of acceptability, but that wouldn't exceed its limits. Except that in the meantime, French society had regressed, and the X rating was instituted in 1975. *A Real Young Girl* wasn't rated X, it was only restricted for those under eighteen, and it received its *visa de sortie*. Then André Génovès and La Boétie Films went bankrupt. Pierre-Richard Muller bought it back so he could exploit it in porno theatres. So no one saw it.

You say something I like very much: before the emergence of the X rating in 1975, filmmakers were concerned with filming both the body and the mind, and afterward, they began to be filmed separately …

Yes, that's obvious. They separated us from the thing that forms our identity. When I'm asked who I am, I'm forced to check off "female." It's always outraged me when I'm asked to identify my sex, because I find that the word necessarily leads to the mental image. From the moment I do that, a pornographic image is integrated into my identity. I don't need to check off my sex.

*"My name is Alice Bonnard, I don't like people, they oppress me."
Your cinema begins with these words. From the beginning, a character who only believes in herself, like all of your heroines: everything
else is unreal. You film French reality like a jinxed nightmare.*

That's what the head of censorship said when he read the
screenplay. He didn't raise an eyebrow at the sexual stuff, it was
the way in which I described, at the beginning of the film, the
woman on the train; I had a take on society that was disagreeable,
contemptuous, I was presenting a terrible image of France. But
that wasn't the subject. My subject was a little girl in the
provinces who hated everything and everyone, except the boy
she liked, whom she ultimately hated, too. The film may have
been wild, but Hiram Keller, whom I had seen in Fellini's
Satyricon, was a star at the time. The grocer is played by Shirley
Stoler from *The Honeymoon Killers* (Leonard Kastle, 1970).
Mort Shuman composed and performed all the music. I don't
think that stars of that stature would have dared or have had the
generosity to make that sort of a film today.

*The film creates an extraterrestrial perspective of the young girl.
Everything appears for the first time. You extend the dimensions of
her body to the dimensions of the world: the vagina, the cerumen
… It's a life-form that you explore in a very clinical way, as if it
were a medical visit. As opposed to a surface fantasy, an imaginary
that doesn't want to see the body with its hairs, its secretions. You
reveal the gore buried in the young girl.*

It's like *eXistenZ* (David Cronenberg, 1999)! An aesthetics of
slime that disgusts us and is intimately tied to the feminine.
That's what Cronenberg understood. I'm certain that he wanted

to do that, reestablish slime as an aesthetic and moral value. My novel *Le soupirail* (The Basement Window) was tightly written, full of metaphorical images.[9] Actually, I have to keep myself from writing alexandrines when I'm writing modern things— for me, the legitimacy of the French language can be found in the alexandrine. So the book is overrun with musical language; it's when I had to make images out of it that it grew very complicated. For example, the little spoon that she sticks in her vagina … How do you film that? How do you ensure that the poetry of the book doesn't become, once it's filmed, prosaic? An image has to have a certain violence.

There's a shot where Alice imagines her father's sex. How do you film that?

Yeah, well, since I wrote it, I had to film it. I always work like that: I write things to force myself to film them. Filming is impossible for me, I'm terrifyingly shy, but I do it anyway because I force myself to, and because it's written in the screenplay. It's impossible for me to do rehearsals because I only film things that I haven't admitted to myself. Everything that I don't want to say and will never say, I film that, I show that, but it remains absolutely violent for me. But that's what being an artist is: saying what no one else says. Art is creating something that no one has ever said. It's transfiguring the banality of all those things that were inculcated in you that were so normative and degrading. I strip myself of it, but always through violence.

---

9. Catherine Breillat, *Le soupirail* (Guy Authier, 1974).

How did you find Charlotte Alexandra, who plays Alice Bonnard?

I saw her in Borowczyk's *Immoral Tales* (1973); she played a young girl who masturbated with a cucumber in the bathroom. I organized a screening of the film for the Musidora collective because I wanted the feminists to support me, but they were totally against the film. They thought it was shameful that a woman would make such a film: "You're supposed to make women's films, you don't have the right to undress women." Actually, yeah, you do have the right. Charlotte came out of the screening with her eyes closed, both arms out in front of her. She went back to England and I never heard from her again.

A Real Young Girl is a very "prepill" imaginary: the terror, the constant fear that something will happen. Everything that happens to her is tied to the fact that the pill doesn't yet exist in France.

All of the moral prohibitions that structured us were in truth only practical prohibitions. That's why the idea was instilled in us of the "first time," which makes us more sentimental than men. You're forced to have a sentimental story in your head when you have sex; that way, if you ever get pregnant, the guy stays attached and you fall into a financial relationship.

The first time exists for men, too.

I don't care!

Back then, how did you know what to do with a man?

I had a boyfriend when I was twelve; he was fourteen, repeating a grade, and he was the best-looking boy in the class. But otherwise, no one knew anything, it was only between girls: a girl who looked at a boy was a prostitute, and a girl who had gotten her period, they said she smelled like fish. If you were found with Tampax, you were accused of not being a virgin anymore, you were found guilty and then they destroyed you. It was a horrible, nightmarish education. Porn films didn't exist, and boys didn't know much more than we did. Which left reading, Lautréamont—Sade I didn't like, but I read him at twelve. I was brilliant at finding the trashiest, most violent stuff. I loved this Audiberti novel where a police chief finds the corpse of a prostitute in a vacant lot and falls in love with her.[10]

What did you do on vacation as a young girl?

I walked in the forest, I collected mushrooms, lots of hazelnuts. I didn't really get along with my sister, I called her "my best required friend." We would have gotten along famously if my mother hadn't taught us to be rivals. Still, we had lots of things in common: the same vocabulary, the same culture, even if we didn't like the same things. Marie-Hélène loved art, prettiness, while I already had brutality in me. I loved to destroy, and I loved shattered beauty. She had a gift for drawing, you don't even know how gifted she was, she was a genius, but she was content with looking pretty, same thing with writing. I was less skilled in drawing, even if I ended up improving through my persistence, so that I could take it all away from her. I had to be

10. Jacques Audiberti, *Marie Dubois* (Gallimard, 1952).

the first even though I was the second, so I had to crush her. But unlike her, I decided to go in the direction of fury. My first oil paintings turned my little twelve-year-old friends into matrons who looked drunk. I painted their characters mercilessly. I loved Soutine. I especially didn't want to be "feminine" in anything I did. I favored force, and therefore frontal brutality. Throwing things in people's faces.

A Real Young Girl is a film that asks, What does a young girl on summer vacation's boredom mean? It's a nightmare, but it also opens up a space in which your cinema will grow.

Basically, what my mother wanted was for us never to go out. She was so afraid that I'd get pregnant because I had gigantic breasts—if only I had cut them off when I was sixteen! When I was eleven, I had a thirty-six-inch bust, we went to Monoprix every month to get a larger size ... We spent those three interminable months in the country. Luckily I was so bored that I read a book a day. That lets you dream, create your own world that protects you from any conditioning. *A Real Young Girl* first had as its title "The Basement Window" because she looks at life that way, almost as if she were buried.

You often return to this detail of breasts as a stigma.

Because it was horrible. I hated men looking at my body, ogling my feminine traits. It was a nightmare, I wanted to be loved for my intelligence.

Is boredom only a thing for young girls, or are you still bored?

I don't think I'm ever bored. Let's just say that boredom is my way of thinking. That gives me an enormous amount of power, it's a way of being with yourself. They say that cinema is a collective art, but it isn't at all: the auteur is alone, absolutely alone. Now, less so, but at the time, a shoot seemed as long to me as when you tell a child that you're leaving for two days— two days is forever. *36 fillette*, despite being short, only six or seven weeks of shooting, seemed interminable to me. I couldn't see the end of it and I was absolutely alone. For everyone else it was Club Med; I hated them because they were fooling around. You make a film alone, you don't have fun. Your actor has to be available: if he's having fun, he'll spoil.

In the film, is the unlucky, incestuous father your own father?

Of course it is, even if I completely invented the incestuous part. And my father was a tall, handsome man. My mother dubbed Hiram Keller's mother. She saw the film and said, "To think that your father won't even be able to recognize himself!" while she recognized herself quite well, and was very proud of having been so smart. My father loved me very much but he was too patronizing. He used to pat my cheek, I hated that. He'd say, "My women"; "I'm a doctor, I have the right to see my three women naked." I couldn't stand hearing it.

It was impossible to see A Real Young Girl *for a long time, right?*

Twenty-five years! The film was stuck at the lab because La Boétie Films went bankrupt. If the film had been shown at the Quinzaine des réalisateurs, it would have come out. But, Luc Moullet assured me, Jacques Poitrenaud and Pierre-Henri

Deleau wanted to interrupt the screening on the pretext that it was pornographic.[11] They wanted to shame the ones who wanted to continue watching something that couldn't possibly be cinema. Cinema has to be appropriate, it has to have good table manners!

I had a screening, and Serge Toubiana, who was running *Cahiers*, thought the film was obscene. He was afraid I would hurt my burgeoning career by showing it—he was really afraid for it and for *Romance*. But I'm intractable, I can't not be me, even if it breaks me. I decided to show it with *Romance* during my retrospective at Rotterdam—two films that are like my alpha and omega—and it was a triumph. Humbert Balsan and I had decided to apply for a "production grant" for a first film: nothing prohibited that, even though the film had been directed twenty-five years earlier. We received €40,000, and were able to pay the lab. A quarter of a century later, the film came out in France and in the world.

The film operates in a very David Hamilton universe, the world of Petit Bateau panties and male fantasy. You seem to begin with that male imaginary, but you do it in order to show that, from the young girl's perspective, it's rotten from the inside.

It isn't really Hamilton at all, I'm much more *trash*! But Petit Bateau was my dream because it was mass-produced, simple, and well made. My grandmother knitted us underpants in mercerized cotton that I was horrified by, my dream was to have underpants in interlock that at the very least wouldn't buckle.

---

11. Jacques Poitrenaud was the director and creator of the Perspectives du cinéma français branch of the Quinzaine des réalisateurs; Pierre-Henri Deleau was in charge of selection for the Quinzaine des réalisateurs from 1969 to 1998.

And Alice doesn't do those languid poses for the photographer's eye, she makes a devastating inventory of that body that's blossoming and oozing from everywhere from her own, unforgiving eye. She's completely clumsy in her body. That's also *A Real Young Girl*, arrogant and naively pretentious as I must have been. Fascinated by the singers on variety shows on TV, an eminently desirable parallel world that she'd like to be a part of. I never interpreted "Annie aime les sucettes" as sleazy.[12]

You never say "woman," you only talk about the young girl. I get the feeling that in your head you never relate to the concept of the adult woman.

[*Girlish laugh*] But that's because it's my favorite cinematic subject! I don't know what a woman is.

The film is such an antidote to the soft-core eroticism of the '70s that I'm surprised that you were also able to write the Bilitis *(1977) screenplay for Hamilton.*

Someone suggested me to David Hamilton. It so happened that I knew him quite well, along with his wife Mona. My husband François Wimille was actually the only man that he ever photographed. I asked an exorbitant price for that screenplay. It could have been good, but to be good Hamilton would have had to make the film with young girls who really were twelve years old. I told Alain Poiré from Gaumont, who at the time only produced family films: "I am an intellectual, Hamilton is

---

12. "Les sucettes" (Lollipops) was a pop song written by Serge Gainsbourg and performed by France Gall (1966). It is full of double entendres that suggest fellatio.

a star photographer; we're the only ones who can afford to use a twelve-year-old girl to play Bilitis, in short to be faithful to Pierre Louÿs's novel." It was revolutionary.

Why did that interest you?

It was forbidden, it was something that had never been done. Except that Hamilton never wanted to do the bare minimum, meaning go and have a meeting with Alain Poiré. He was obsessed with his photographs and his light, which he could only find in Ramatuelle and Cap d'Agde. He was a gentle, elegant man who barely ever talked but was monomaniacal and probably not all there, mentally. He spent all of his vacations at Cap d'Agde, in this paradise of young Nordic girls who don't have the same relationship to their bodies as we do at all: they were already naked, all you had to do was make them put on some Petit Bateau underpants that were a size too large, so they would nonchalantly gape at the crotch. David only worked with natural light and with a great deal of precision. At the very last moment, he would breathe on the lens to get that gauzy effect, that was his secret. Sylvio Tabet was the one who ultimately produced the film. Alain Terzian was his assistant; he was very young. When I demanded to be paid for my screenplay, he said to me, "A beautiful girl like you can live, she doesn't need to ask for money." That threw me into a mad rage, probably excessively so. I hated him, I always hated him, that lecherous creep.

You did Bilitis *for the money?*

Yes. But I make a commission my own. And I thought I'd have more influence on the film. Although I did manage to convince

Hamilton to use Bernard Giraudeau. David didn't think he was handsome enough, and very much preferred the catastrophe that was Gilles Kohler. The film is awful, contrived, tasteless. A school-play version of Shakespeare isn't Shakespeare. And since Poiré was no longer around, Bilitis wasn't twelve anymore, but twenty. The actress, Patti D'Arbanville, wore those vile braids to make her look younger. That was the end! When you're twelve, and proud as a peacock, there's something magical in that. You have to make the film with young, innocent girls. You need me at twelve. The film is just silly ... It's long-winded, there's nothing there, not a single scene. There's only pathetic male fantasies and a vulgarity that's just atrocious. But it sold a lot of tickets.

After Bilitis, *you wrote the screenplay for* Catherine & Co., *with Jane Birkin. Did you enjoy it, did you make money... ?*

I think I prostituted myself with that script. For a long time people thought that I was a good screenwriter and that it was better if real, professional directors made the films that I was writing. But those films, they were written for me. It's writerly prostitution because it's me every time, I always use myself and my life in my writing. Shouldn't I have been the one who made *Le Diable au corps* (Gérard Vergez, 1990)? I stopped writing for other people when I was officially able to make a film. I earned a lot of money from it, I was writing up to six scripts at once. I enjoyed it but, like always, you immediately blow the money you make by playing the prostitute, so it's useless. By using my literary talent in the service of cinema, I lost the thread with books. But maybe I should have done more to earn a living and feed my kids.

How did you end up acting in Bertolucci's Last Tango in Paris *(1972)?*

My father wanted to bring us to Niort, in the Deux-Sèvres, because it had become clear that we weren't taking classes in oriental languages—our original excuse for moving to Paris. I managed to convince him to enroll us in the Furet school, in a course for the dramatic arts, so we could stay in Paris. Right away, I was discovered by Jean-Gabriel Albicocco to play Yvonne de Galais in *The Wanderer*, which didn't happen, or rather, it happened without me![13] My sister played Bernadette Soubirous.[14] She was well paid and started getting enough money to buy an apartment. I had nothing. It was extremely painful. At seventeen, I had become her sad sister, the one who didn't succeed. That's what pushed me to write *L'homme facile*. I absolutely had to write, to be published, for there to be some separation between the two sisters. And after all, I had the passion to succeed. In the meantime, Bertolucci was looking for twins, and we were "the Breillat twins"—I forced my sister to go and she was really angry with me since it was just a shitty little role.

Do you remember the shoot?

I learned on that shoot that hideous, lousy dialogue can be completely transformed through camera movement. The dialogue was by Agnès Varda, shitty feminist dialogue. But what a cinematic lesson for me! We had rehearsed with Maria, in a

---

13. It was ultimately Brigitte Fossey who played Yvonne de Galais in Jean-Gabriel Albicocco's *The Wanderer* (1967).
14. *L'affaire Lourdes* (1967), a film for television made by Marcel Bluwal.

café, "Marriage, that's not for me. Maybe when I'll have to add sugar to strawberries," an extremely grotesque line. But suddenly, with Bertolucci's mise-en-scène and Vittorio Storaro's dancerly camera, all of that was transcended. It wasn't three stuck-up women spouting feminist absurdities in a café anymore, something else was there, a kind of poetic outline.

It's strange, and at the same time very consistent, that your name is affiliated with all of these works and artists who have now been cancelled: Hamilton's Bilitis, *Bertolucci's* Last Tango in Paris ...

I neither defend Hamilton nor condemn him. I didn't witness what some people are accusing him of. It was an era. He contributed something that seduced the entire world; *Hamiltonian* became an adjective. But that's diametrically opposed to my vision as a director. I like ultra-sharp images, and leave no space for poetic blur. But Bertolucci, I'll defend him tooth and nail, he's a great director. I was there for *Last Tango*. The stick of butter wasn't the problem. It was purely symbolic, there was no pornography there. Only at the time, the symbolism was very violent. The day after the scene, the entire dressing room— makeup, hair, etc.—did nothing but whisper. The whispers became rumors and rumors are always devastating. Maria Schneider was pursued by all of these people who thought they were allowed to openly laugh at her. People would routinely place a stick of butter in front of her on the table in restaurants. That's what destroyed her. Not the making of the film. And now, these same people portray themselves as the bestowers of morality and virtue?

As for Maruschka Detmers, she wasn't devastated by that blow job in *Devil in the Flesh* (Marco Bellocchio, 1986), which was done in private. What wrecked Marutschka, she told me, wasn't the scene itself—she could handle it—but everyone who, afterward, only wanted to talk about that, and who reduced her to someone who gives blow jobs. It's not the films or the directors who are guilty, but the people they reveal … These new mini-Savonarolas who think that they're vested with a judicial mission, and are currently rearing their hideous heads in the name of a retroactive moral rigor. To get back to Bellocchio, I think if you're doing an intimate scene that's going to be shown in a film, then you can't start saying to actors, "No one's there, don't worry." It would be crude to do that to actors. No, everyone needs to be there, because it will be presented to the world. If there's a film crew there, you understand that it's work. Taking away the whole crew in order to make the actors comfortable would be a mistake. I've always shot intimate scenes with around at least eight people: the camera crew, mise-en-scène, and sound, and within earshot, makeup and hair. That way, it's assumed that it's public. And not a private thing at all.

Do you keep a journal, like Alice does?

No. My journal is in my head, that's much more effective. All those moments, those scenes, those dialogues that I've carefully observed forever and stored up in my head like a computer, I can conjure them up at will. My films are deeply autobiographical, from beginning to end. I invent practically nothing. Oddly enough, *Abuse of Weakness* is almost the least autobiographical of my films. Ōshima said that the more a director hides behind fiction, the more she reveals herself. And that inversely, the more she desires to present herself, the more she hides. I hide myself, too; I always change social class, for example.

For *A Real Young Girl*, I chose that setting, Landes, because it was a young girl's dream: those pine trees, that sticky resin … those straight, graphic trunks that diffract that insane light. And I love the devastated beauty you see in that film: a garbage dump lining the beach, the carcasses of dead dogs. Beauty isn't cinematographic, but ugliness is.

Are you always working to shatter beauty?

Yes, fundamentally that's the artistic gesture I love best. But sometimes I don't manage to do it. When I finished *Romance*, I was distraught, I could see that I'd made a film that was icy, that had a glacial beauty, and I immediately wanted to start over so that I could make it in the mud, and not in the ether. That's why I made *Anatomy of Hell*, except that I made that one in the ether, too—I'm incorrigible.

What do you mean by "mud"?

"Mud" means a destroyed, shattered, dirtied, violated beauty. That's spectacular and deeply moving. *Destroy, She Said.* I adore that Duras title, but I didn't read the book. For me, life is also disaster, romantic destruction. *Les Chants de Maldoror*, always.

Where does that penchant come from?

It's literary, above all else. With the twenty-six letters of the alphabet, you travel all over the world, through every country, every era, every sex. You're a man, you're a woman, you feel every emotion. You kill, you are killed, you fuck without restriction. You're free. That's how I was formed, by binge reading.

Lautréamont was the first and only one I loved. And then Henry Miller, Audiberti, Ellroy, that violence against women that's sexual, they don't hide any of it. I like the violence of men against women if they're great writers. The abominable misogyny of Henry Miller doesn't hurt me. When I read, I become him. I don't identify with his partners but with him, the writer. I don't care about artistic misogyny, the only thing that's ever hurt me is inequality. That the director of the IDHEC could have told my father that he couldn't accept me in the directorial department because I would end up unemployed. But screen-writing or editing, that was OK. A nurse, but not a doctor! Why? Balls aren't cerebral hemispheres. I'm not feminine, but feminist, and I like artistic violence: Saint Anthony pierced by arrows always inspired me. It's magnificent. Beauty ought to be cruel and frightening.

So you need to avoid not only the beautiful but also the eroticism that you've always hated. How do you avoid that?

André Génovès called me to do a feminine erotic film, as if I were Régine Deforges, even though I'm just the opposite. I don't know what eroticism is. It's empty, it's bodies that are bodies and nothing more. With *Emmanuelle* (Just Jaeckin, 1974), there's no story, no soul, nothing. You have to put human feeling, human life into it: Is it about pleasure, *jouissance*, denigration, the wounds that one inflicts on oneself?

You mean that you have to show the consequences? When I think about it, you always show the consequences of a sexual relationship.

Always. I didn't know that was it, but you're right.

That carries weight; it's not just imagery, there are consequences.

For me, it's harsh, whatever it is. The things people claim to be the dirtiest and most crude can reach the divine. That's why society has to mutilate them, it's absolutely impossible that we could learn that the sexual path could be a divine path, the royal path of absolute transparency. Know thyself: be lucid, see the self, understand the self … I want to see myself, to film what is never shown except in a pornographic or erotic way. While something totally different, something important in a different way, is playing out. Quite simply, the meaning of life.

WITH
NOTHING

Nocturnal Uproar • every time I made a film, I lost the man I was with • Pygmalions for actresses • women filmmakers are supposed to be ugly • I crossed social classes • life kills you on its own • I don't want to die of shame • worse than Max Pécas • you can't take away my life from me • I am the film • the director's objective enemy • off to the 24 Heures du Man • be Catherine Deneuve • the Stradivarius who won't sleep with you • between the boundary and the limit • *Police* and *Dirty like an Angel* • the cursed filmmaker with the most money • otherwise you wouldn't even get up in the morning • I could put televisions everywhere

Murielle Joudet: *Solange (Dominique Laffin), the heroine of* Nocturnal Uproar, *is a very engaged, sexually liberated Parisian woman: she's making a film, she has lovers, she lives by night ...* A Real Young Girl *was the waking nightmare of a body that didn't belong. The film that follows it is a nocturnal dream, a woman's paradise: it's the end of the '70s, a postpill and pre-AIDS world. It's intoxicating.*

Catherine Breillat: I wanted to make a comedy of manners, a little like *Annie Hall* (Woody Allen, 1977), that would have an *A Woman Is a Woman* (Jean-Luc Godard, 1961) side to it. I find that everything modern is at the same time very fussy, and I've always loved that. I adore mannered women and I wanted to make a film about one. At the end of the Godard, when they talk to each other through the interposed titles of books, it's simultaneously very mannered, hypercorrect, and full of wit. I was also thinking about *Looking for Mr. Goodbar* (Richard Brooks, 1977). That starts with a very light, comedic tone and gradually sinks into something more serious, which lots of viewers couldn't stand in my film: the masochistic side of that unhealthy relationship that is, simultaneously, a quest for self.

What was your situation after A Real Young Girl, *in the middle of the '70s?*

I had broken into the scene, and immediately made lots of friends; I knew everyone in Paris, all the important people, everyone. I understood what the CNC was, that you had to apply for an advance on receipts and get into the business. The advance on receipts for *Nocturnal Uproar* was incredible: I was recounting my Parisian love affairs, and people recognized themselves, particularly Benoît Jacquot and Daniel Toscan du Plantier, who were on the committee. They were dead set against the film being made. Hubert Astier, the president of the organization, is the one who got it for me. It's always like that: when some people are against you, others appear who are totally for you. Also, I remember that when I saw that they were giving money to mediocre film-makers, I said, "Look at the photo of the director: the screenplay is terrible, his films are terrible, but he still has money. Look at the photo! They're little hustlers! Guys get money that way, too."

And the women?

Women filmmakers are supposed to be ugly. And incidentally, that was my problem. I'm not beautiful anymore, but I really used to be. Every time I made a film, I lost the man I was with. It was unbearable for them: they wanted to help a woman become an actress, be Pygmalions for actresses, but not female directors.

What happened with your partners, specifically?

A film means total absorption: the world could fall apart. I remember having to fight to call my kids and read the news. A shoot doesn't last long because I film at breakneck speed, but it lasts too long for men to forgive you. They all wanted to play Willy to my Colette.[15] Or at least give advice, participate. That's impossible for me. I violently exclude them.

---

15. Henry Gauthier-Villars, aka Willy, Colette's first husband, took not only the credit for the *Claudine* series but also the revenue from those hit novels whose rights he sold in his own name. He published more than fifty novels, the majority of which were written by ghostwriters. Jules Renard said of him, "Willy *have* a lot of talent."

I need to be centered, concentrated on myself and the film. It's a ruthless face-off, where there isn't any room for their paternalism. A shoot is absolutely solitary; I don't even speak to the actors, except during takes. The only people who belong there are the ones on set making the film with me. The friends and lovers who couldn't be discouraged from dropping by to see us on set are like strangers who get in the way.

During editing, there's less pressure, and my private life gradually falls back into place, but not like before. I don't think they understand that kind of ruthless exclusion. They have this fantasy that they're Pygmalions, even though they're of no use to you.

Could the class differences between you and your husbands have been a problem?[16] *Did that create an imbalance?*

I'm very sensitive about this subject. I came from nothing and became a filmmaker. I never experienced that problem of social differences in a relationship. It's the kids who, afterward, prefer the family that gives them a social advantage. My mothers-in-law, all of whom came from the most prominent French families, always adored me. Even after the breakups, I still considered them my family, to the point that I abandoned the whole idea of my own family. I didn't have a problem crossing social classes. Quite the opposite, I always gave up trying to get my hooks into a rich man. I didn't have to try, actually, because they were the ones who came looking for me, and I just had to let it happen. You can be rich and still be very desirable.

---

16. Breillat was married three times: to François Wimille, Emmanuel Schlumberger, and Stéphane Magnard.

Wait, why do you oppose the two?

If you fall in love with a rich man, they'll say you love him because he's rich, but no: it's because he's handsome, intelligent, and, cherry on top, he has money. My husbands had it all and that annoyed me. I knew that with my horrible laziness, I wouldn't be able to do anything if my husband started financing my films. I would have gotten like Marie Antoinette, intoxicated by the abominable and seriously enjoyable futility of money, but I had to hold on to the harshness of life.

How do you keep a balance? How do you not end up on the street, while holding on to the harshness of life?

I never stayed with any of them for very long. I've lived my life as a tightrope walker, an equilibrist. Sometimes I didn't even dare walk past my bank because I had so little money. I remember one day when I went with my young daughter for her to get a visa, I found a bundle of cash on the steps of the Métro that was enough money for me to live on until my next film.

The question of money was never a source of anxiety for you?

Sure, but not to the point that I worried myself to death over it. I take risks, all the time, in my life and in my art. But I always tell myself that tomorrow is another day, that I always have time to kill myself. You always have time, and plus, life kills you on its own, you don't have to preempt it. It's not worth it. I've always been saved by miracles, I've had staggering fears about money but I overcame them, I don't know how—by holding fast. It ain't over 'til it's over. I'm stoic, you can't even imagine how stoic I am. I'm highly resistant to everything.

Do you think that your films have always been underfunded?

Yes, always, because in spite of everything, I didn't enter the star system. I think that these days, being a woman counts for very little. But at the time, back when I was starting out, not only was I a woman, but I was going on men's turf and approaching subjects that were normally off-limits to women. Women had to be pretty, sentimental, modest. But I like ugliness, I don't want to die of shame. Unpacking ugliness, I find that very, very beautiful. Or perhaps very, very great.

How do you present ugliness in a film?

With *A Real Young Girl*, I decided that I wouldn't use French colors, which were fashionable at the time. All of French cinema was predominantly beige or blue. I decided that the film would be multicolored, garish, that we would have a trailer covered in orange carpet that was in at the time, the ugliest thing in the world. I hadn't ever been inside a trailer but I had wanted to confront that horrible universe people lived in. I sewed Alice's T-shirt myself, it was turquoise, a color that was considered to be awful, and I added this absurd braided white rickrack to the collar. I dyed the bathing suit pink and black. I hate good taste—that belongs in a bourgeois salon, not in art. The only concern that the French censor had with *A Real Young Girl* was about my very negative opinion of the French population.

That hatred of France …

France is sycophantic and hypocritical and, what's even worse, the slogan of the French Revolution is "Liberty, Equality, Fraternity for all men," meaning no woman will ever be their equal. It's France's founding principle, the only country where royalty applied the Salic law: women can't reign. Queens everywhere, except in France. They'd rather go and find some distant, hated cousin than have a woman rule. The hatred for women in France runs deep, so deep that they guillotined a revolutionary like Olympe de Gouges. Misogyny is in France's DNA.

Those three traits, do you find them still today?

Yes, yes, even in cinema. To get financing, you have to do a lot of lobbying and you have to be a hypocrite: you pretend that something bad is good, there's constant backscratching ... But, OK, maybe it's like that in every country in the world. It's impossible for me to say something's good when I don't think it's any good. I can get around it a bit by saying that a little microscopic thing is good in a film that I don't like, but that's it.

Was Nocturnal Uproar *well received?*

No, I was the worst director the world had ever seen. Worse than Max Pécas, worse than anyone. The worst in the world. One critic wrote that I should keep writing instead of making films. The only review that wasn't devastating was Pascal Bonitzer's in *Cahiers du cinéma*. Everyone in Paris knew that the film was about Toscan and Jacquot. Pascal Thomas also recognized himself. It was insane, the level of visceral hate. Why so much hatred for very small films that say very intimate things about very minor things? It was considered the worst French film of the year. *36 fillette*, same thing. I was the disgrace of France.

When you use actors to portray your relatives, do you think about the reaction that will provoke?

Christian Bourgois warned me. He said, "It's crazy, everyone who hangs out with writers must know that they will, to some extent, show up in their work. They blame you not only because they recognize themselves, but because on top of that, it isn't really them." Obviously: you steal something from them and at the same time, it isn't them, that's the problem when you draw from your own life. Bergman, Proust, Miller: they did the same thing. You have no choice. My films are profoundly autobiographical and yet not that autobiographical: I amalgamate eras, one person with another, then I'll add a news story. I don't invent anything, just the order. I rearrange, but I don't invent anything.

I always wonder how you're expected to have enough confidence and authority on your first couple of shoots. Don't you ask yourself, "Will the actress be able to handle playing that?" How do you manage other people's subjectivities?

What do you mean, "other people's subjectivities"? The actress? The important thing is that she's good, that she isn't ashamed of the film, and that I'm not either. I don't care about niceties, I don't have time. You have to pull the image out from the void. The only thing I ask myself is how I'm going to get through this. That's the existential question that, for me, takes up all the space. I told Etienne Chicot, whom I didn't get along with at all on *36 fillette* and who wanted to pull rank, that he was the just the ink I used to make my films, that's all. Actually, I prefer nonactors, I call them "nascent oxygen." Like Anaïs Reboux (*Fat Girl*), like Caroline Ducey (*Romance*) … They give themselves to the camera completely, there's no reticence, unlike professional actors. I have a universe I draw everyone into, a universe that no one talks about but that concerns everyone. I know that I have that power of conviction, because deep down, it's my life that's at stake—you can't take my life away from me.

You've already asked yourself, "How far can I go with that power?"

No, because I don't know how I'm doing it, so I can't use it like power. The problem is how to hold on by something other than male authority. I know that I have immense power on set, but I don't get it by being authoritative. I understood very quickly that, on a shoot, when you speak softly, people are forced to be quiet and listen. I'm dictatorial, and yet I don't give orders. I am totally committed to my film and it's like people are magnetized, they become me. If you give orders, they'll resist, they don't want to or can't do what's asked of them. The order incapacitates them, it's a reflex. The crew always loves me because they understand what I'm doing. It's the technicians who are closest to the film. The cinematographer, too, but he's so preoccupied by his lighting that he gets tangled up in his personal egocentrism, which keeps him from getting completely fascinated by the film and the way in which I shake up the actors. During the shoot of *Fat Girl*, I said, "It's simple, I don't *make* the film, I don't make anything." Everyone else *makes*: the cinematographer, the sound engineer, the stage hands … Whereas I *am* the film. The actors don't make the film, they are *made* in the film. They're wrapped up in my gaze, as if I had thrown out a net. They need to be me, they start to resemble me.

There's always a rivalry between the director and the director of photography, isn't there?

Yes, actually I have this aphorism that I like, I say that he's the director's objective enemy. There's something so immaterial about the work of mise-en-scène ...

How do you resolve that relationship between intimate enemies? Does that interest you?

I love having authority over a chauvinist. Now, the crew, that's another story, they have to follow and even slightly anticipate the actors' movements during a tracking shot, so they're much more attuned to the sensibility of the film. They always forgive me for everything I do with the actors because they know what I'm striving for. But you can't ever be gratuitously mean or unfair with actors, otherwise you'll upset the whole crew.

Where is the limit? From the actor's point of view, there may be no difference between malice and a harshness that serves the film.

Even when they're furious, even when I "torture" them on set, when we get that magical take, I can assure you that they're very proud of themselves. They might hate me, but they're happy. Even Léa Drucker (*Last Summer*), who is exceptionally sweet, told me that I tortured her. I would say to her, "No! You raised your eyebrows, you batted your eyes, I don't want that! ..." "No, you're doing Delphine Seyrig, I love Seyrig but not in this film," "That's Chekhov ... Greta Garbo raised an eyebrow, but the rest of the face has to be like ice." French actresses act, but I want them to *be*. When Léa was acting, I told her that she was ugly and that I wanted her to be beautiful, because otherwise it wouldn't be credible that a seventeen-year-old boy would be in love with her.

It's hard to hear that, especially for an actress.

Yes, but I explained my vocabulary to her: "When I tell you you're beautiful, it's because you're acting well! It's simple, when you act well, you're beautiful. The face lights up, it expands. When I tell you you're ugly, it's because you're acting badly, you're making faces that make you ugly." That goes for the men as well, Olivier Rabourdin (*Last Summer*) heard the same thing—to be an actor, you have to be stoic. Getting into the film is violent. Nobody knows each other, you don't know your actors, they don't know you, they're afraid, and fear is disfiguring. You don't know what film you're making yet. It's like animals: they have to sniff around, jostle each other a bit, learn to speak the same language. And then two days later, even if you have to remain vigilant, I'd say that the film directs itself. Once you've understood how it works, it's off to the 24 Heures du Mans. They're radiant in the end, and they don't need any compliments for that. I never give them. The entire set is radiant: that's the real compliment. The real happiness.

I think I wasn't like that with Samuel Kircher because he didn't have any tics; it was his first film. I told him to learn the text inside and out, to rehearse it while he was exercising, that way he wouldn't be acting, he'd be doing something else. I adore actors who have never shot a film. They give themselves over to the film, they haven't a single tic, a single fear, they just simply give themselves over. It's dazzling. During editing, though, I did notice that I harangued him, too. I always wanted excellence.

Great filmmakers are always wary of professional actors: Bruno Dumont, Alain Guiraudie, Abdellatif Kechiche, you …

Yes, because you have to dare to work with them. Getting financing for a film depends so much on stars that you don't dare say to them, "That's terrible, I want you to do nothing!" I say, "Be Catherine Deneuve, she doesn't do anything, that's what's good about it. She talks, that's it. She doesn't do anything but talk, nothing else. And it's great."

You said somewhere that actors are prostitutes, what does that mean?

You mustn't understand that sexually, but as it was understood in eighteenth-century France: actors were considered prostitutes because they felt real emotions, which they ranted about in public, and because their bodies were the tools they used to do their work. That's not a moral judgement, it's a fact. They're not simulating anything, so it's prostitution. But it's a sacred kind of prostitution, prostitution for art. There will always be bad faith assholes who say, "Breillat said actors are prostitutes." But who wouldn't want to be prostituted for art?

Let's just say that could lead to confusion; people might think that means "casting couch."

I've never slept with my actors, I don't believe in it. You don't get anything out of doing that, either. When you do tests with a hundred people, there's only one who is made for your film. You think Pialat didn't want to sleep with Sandrine Bonnaire, that he wasn't sick that she didn't want him? She was the only one who could do that film, and he chose her. When you're not the rare pearl, then yeah, if you're on the couch, you have that "extra" something that means that the producer or director who hasn't found the rare pearl might prefer to use you. But when you come across a James Dean or a Sandrine Bonnaire, you're willing to restrain yourself, to suffer the agony. The actor who is made for you could despise you, think you're ugly, flout you, make you suffer, you'd still choose them, that I'm sure of. You really have to think that actors have no talent to think that sex will open doors for you. It misunderstands cinema, thinking that actors are nobodies. Actors are Stradivariuses. When the miracle of discovering one happens, even though the fiddle will sleep with you, well, you pick the Stradivarius who won't sleep with you.

I'm realizing that all the French filmmakers I love are dealing with some kind of madness. I wonder if that's not the secret …

But I say it myself that I'm crazy. I know I am. If only for my obstinacy for doing impossible things. I reread the screenplay for *Anatomy of Hell* and it was complete madness. Why would you do that? How could I write that for myself, force myself to make it? It's horrendous. I know that I'm crazy. Jean-François Lepetit was sick that I wanted to make that film before *The Last Mistress* (*Une vieille maîtresse*), which risked compromising its viability, and making me a total pariah again. But I couldn't not do it. My concept was that it was a film meant for museums, not for cinema audiences. I had fourteen copies pulled from the negative to get the color exactly right. Like a painter. Pulling fourteen copies from a negative is total madness.

And in daily life, do you become normal again?

I'm still a bit crazy. I'll buy anything, anyway. I'll buy a house in a second, without thinking about it at all. I'll buy anything, but I know what I buy will be beautiful. With food, with everything. It's simple, there's no limit. When it's a matter of spending, I go to the limit of what I can do, hence of what I can't do.

What have you bought recently?

I bought some stunning earrings. But I have to get my ears pierced!

It's a little like your films: you do what you're not allowed to do.

My films are located between the boundary and the limit. The boundary is what people are supposed to tolerate at any given moment, but just barely. That's their limit, but it isn't mine. I'm in a *no-man's-land* that's located after the boundary, but before the limit. After the boundary, it's my cinema. And I don't even go to the limit, I don't cross that—I'm not making *snuff movies*, after all.

The madness of filmmakers seems really tied to a denial of the real that's very strong, a way of bucking it, of forcing it open.

Saying that you're making a film is already a refusal of the real. You don't have a penny to make it with, but you have to tell yourself you're going to make it so that you can raise the money—just barely, but you end up raising it. You have to refuse the real in order to make films that aren't made for the market. If you want to make a product for the market and use "*bankable*" actors that are pushed on you by the big agencies, and television producers give you money … then you're not in denial of the real.

How did you come to write the screenplay for Police, *for Maurice Pialat?*

Initially, Pialat wanted to adapt *L'intérimaire* (1982), Brigitte Lozerec'h's autobiography, in which she tells the story of how her brothers forced her to sleep with them. He was going to use Huppert in the leading role and wanted me to write the screenplay. And then Depardieu called, he was angry with Maurice but after watching *Loulou* (1980) again, he really liked it, and wanted to make another film with him soon. So, *exit* Huppert … Then they turned to *Police*, which, at the beginning, was called "L'étreinte" (The embrace).

It was originally a novel?

Yes, he thought that his favorite book, *À nos amours!* (P. J. Wolfson, 1931), whose title he had already used, could be used as a framework for a men's film. Unfortunately, it's a novel about the American police and American gangsters, so it's nearly impossible to adapt to the French system. Still, I started writing the screenplay. I was supposed to focus on the female character while a journalist from *Le Monde*, who specialized in French detective stories, was going to write the male part, but nothing came out of that. So in the end, it was just me who wrote everything, based on the book. Cut to Cannes where, in the middle of lunch, Depardieu asks how things are going with the screenplay. Toscan says that I'm working on it, that it's wonderful and that Maurice is very pleased … But I didn't have anything, I hadn't written anything yet, so I claimed that the script was unreadable in the state it was in. That night I went to see Martine Offroy, who was in charge of the Série Noire at

Gallimard,[17] and I told her, "Listen, Martine, we have to find another Série Noire, this one is unadaptable." She said that was impossible. I was completely alone, the book was unadaptable, I can only write what I know, and I don't know cops. But I did know a lawyer who was a bit of a sham, and completely bonkers (he was played by Anconina). I told her that the film was a little like Hemingway's *The Old Man and the Sea*: taking out a boat and thinking that you're going to bring back the biggest fish in the world. But what the hell, I had to try.

You were hired to write Sophie Marceau's part and you ended up writing the whole thing, and since you have no imagination, you went out into the field.

On my own initiative I went to the Fourth Brigade Territoriale, the territorial brigades, with plain-clothed policemen in the field. That had never been explored in cinema before. I showed up on their turf saying that I wanted to make a film. At first, they acted like "movie policemen," but once I had stayed there from morning until night they started acting normal again and ended up forgetting about me. I saw it all. A gangster's lawyer took me to the café of the boss of the Tunisian heroin trade in Paris. I spent entire nights there. I knew all the cases and little by little, I saw all the gangsters. In the morning I would go to Maurice's to tell him all about it, and independently started writing what would become *Dirty like an Angel* (*Sale comme un ange*).

What happened with Pialat?

---

17. Gallimard's series of crime novels.

I think that he had in his head that he would write the screenplay and I'd only be there to tell him what I saw. It couldn't be a woman's screenplay because it had to be a men's film. Nor could it be a written screenplay, because Maurice wanted it to be his—that, I understood at my own expense. The film was to be presented at the Venice Film Festival without my name in the credits. Pialat didn't want it, and Gaumont was stuck. There was also the book that I had written based on my research. Albin Michel wanted to publish it and Pialat wanted to be coauthor. I told him, "Maurice, I've never needed a pimp." At two in the morning, I was still at my lawyer's, with Nicolas Seydoux from Gaumont on one end of the line and Richard Ducousset from Albin Michel on the other. We ended up coming to a grotesque agreement: they'd say that I had the original idea, I'd have 75 percent of the SACD royalties, and Albin Michel could put the film's poster on the cover of the book—a poster featuring actors whose names I wasn't allowed to utter. I did 90 percent of the script, Maurice nothing. Well, he made the film, and that's fine: I don't think that you're stealing from a screenwriter when you make a film from his script, the film is the film. But it was my screenplay. Even if, in the end, Sophie Marceau gives the money back. I guess Maurice and Jacques Fieschi together don't make a man's film, but a wimpy film. It's self-righteous, ludicrous nonsense. If the actual girl had given the money back, she'd be dead. But she took off with the cop and they never found her. She gave them the finger. Isn't that a better ending?

Why did you want to make your own version?

I found the screenplay and wanted to throw it away but when I reread it, I realized that it was good. I knew cops and crooks so well. I had been totally immersed in their world. Crooks and lawyers at night, cops during the day. The defense attorney who announced "All of my clients are guilty!" and who, generally, based his cases on technicalities, as if it were a game of chess between him and the cops. It was a surprisingly well-knit microcosm, they were all friends. I brought many of the actual protagonists to the shoot, to replace the actors they had cast at the last minute, since they were awful. But still, there are things that Pialat did much better than me and other things that I did much better than him. In *Dirty like an Angel*, the scene where Brasseur takes Lio home in the car, it's the same as in *Police*.

What did Pialat do better than you?

Depardieu is, after all, a better actor than Brasseur.

What do you think about À nos amours *(Maurice Pialat, 1983)?*

There are two extraordinary things about it: Maurice is a very good actor, and then there's Sandrine. But I still find it a bit lazy, it's not tight, or sharp, but it has charm. I don't understand the stature that Maurice has compared to Jacques Doillon, who never had any money. Pialat was swimming in money, he was the most spoiled "cursed" filmmaker in France, and he never stopped complaining even though he had more money, more shooting days, and more latitude than anyone else. I'm not saying Pialat is bad, but that Doillon could easily claim the same stature. I'd like to see *Les Doigts dans la tête* (1974) again, which I liked a lot. It seems to me that Doillon made important films with nothing. With nothing, once again.

That interests you, making something from nothing?

Yes, that way everyone's on the same level. Doillon is on that level. Pialat, no.

It's as if it's a cheat.

Yes.

And if you had a ton of money?

When I've screwed up a scene, normally I don't have the means to redo it. That said, I'm an emergency filmmaker, I have to be up against the wall. That's where I transcend myself, and reveal myself. If you were to give me too much time and too much money, I might be mediocre.

Did you miss working on shoots?[18]

I'd prefer to do that exclusively. On *Last Summer*, Saïd Ben Saïd stripped me of all my usual support. The film had to be made according to his conditions, so he fired everyone. I didn't have my old assistant, no one. It gave me absolute freedom because I realized that I didn't need anyone, that all of those people who had been working with me for twenty years had made me think they were indispensable.

You felt a difference?

---

18. Breillat didn't make a film for almost ten years, between *Abuse of Weakness* (2013) and *Last Summer* (2023).

Lightness. My assistant made my work schedule because I never understand anything. I don't know how long it takes me to shoot and I can't imagine it, that's the way it is. Everyone always told me about their algorithms, their editing scores … such nonsense that made me think that you had to know me to work with me. I realized that wasn't true. Gabrièle [Roux], my assistant on the film, would simply say to me "Don't worry, it's my job," and not "I have to adapt to you because you're so special." I realized that people were just doing their job.

What would you do on your Breillat island?

Basically, nothing. If Saïd hadn't come looking for me, nothing, I wouldn't have done anything, even the book I have to do. You live from day to day without worrying about death for one second, otherwise you wouldn't even get up in the morning. You waste your time as best you can, I'm the first one to do that. I could do more things, write more, for example, write what I have to write before I die, but it's clear that I'm going to die first. But it would be great if I could do it. I don't want to rest, but I don't do anything. I look at the sea, I watch television, I could put televisions everywhere. I'll watch anything, people talking. I love watching people talking, and I think, "I'd like to shoot that one." As you know, I find actors everywhere.

And in this apartment?

Well, television. But I don't write. How do you expect me to write on a desk in front of a wall? That's not possible. I can't write in front of a wall.

LOVE
IN FRANCE

Perfect Love • the Belfort case • I must have murder
fantasies • Alain Soral, who just made me want to
vomit • people want to see themselves, they want to
make movies • I abhor beginnings • I was thinking
Japanese • fifty stab wounds, that's delirious • when I
take stock of my loves and passions, it's laughable
• men see us as their possessions • falling in love
isn't even normal • if you're equal, you're not making
love • total surrender of the magnificent, primordial
stud • *Bad Love* • there's an innocence about me
when it comes to scandal • I know it's possible to
love a beast • someone like me, who has always
lived with her fists clenched

Murielle Joudet: Perfect Love *begins at the end of the story, with a reenactment of the murder scene with investigators followed by on-camera testimony by the daughter of the victim.*

Catherine Breillat: I copied a real reenactment that was in *L'amour en France,*[19] a documentary about the Belfort murder: a man sodomized his girlfriend with a dustpan handle before killing her by stabbing her fifty times. The interview with the victim's daughter is also authentic; I copied the whole thing word for word. She said she knew she should blame the man, but she couldn't bring herself to because he had made her mother happy. I find that fascinating, the idea of a killer being a lover. I must have murder fantasies.

Why open with this reenactment?

Because it was real and I'm fascinated by the real. And plus, once you've seen the reenactment and know what happened, it's surprising to watch the love story unfold. That also allowed me to be much less graphic and much more allusive when I was filming the moment of the crime.

How did you choose the actors, Isabelle Renauld and Francis Renaud, to play the couple?

Francis Renaud had made a film he was very good in, which wasn't the case on *Perfect Love,* where he was clumsy, stilted, like a peacock, this little macho guy ... it was unbelievable. You had to torture him to get him to act; otherwise, he would just strut

---

19. A ten-episode documentary series made by Daniel Karlin and Tony Lainé, broadcast on Antenne 2 (1990).

around the set. He slept with the actress, the makeup artist … And he absolutely wanted to sleep with me, except that I never sleep with my actors, thank God! He still found a way to tell everyone that he had slept with me, the little braggart.

Why the title, Perfect Love?

Because at first those two spun the perfect love affair, but then they spun out. My heroines are often psychologically dominated by men. Not in this case: she's the stronger one, in the victim's role. Why does he murder her? She mocks him and his lack of virility, and that's what he murders. He murders her laughter. If she had stopped laughing in time, she'd still be alive. In those types of cases, you have to stop laughing right away. I'm sure that's what happened to Marie Trintignant, she kept talking. Men kill us because women verbalize much better than they do, and say things that they can't bear to hear. They kill us to make us stop talking. In the film, he murders laughter. To kill laughter, you need five hundred stab wounds, not two, not three. Laughter is inextinguishable.

How did Alain Soral end up in the film?

Stéphane [Magnard], my son Paul's father, was very good friends with Alain Soral, who just made me want to vomit. I'd had dinner with them when I was shooting *Dirty like an Angel*. I was pregnant, and Soral dared say to me, looking me straight in the eyes, that women are nothing but wombs, that they're only made to procreate. Then he went into an insane rant about Jews being everywhere, Jewish money, the Jews that were keeping him from writing … It was a nightmare. Totally revolting.

What kept him from writing was his laziness and total lack of talent. That night, I started to have agonizing contractions. The next day, I was shooting the cemetery scene in *Dirty like an Angel*, but I couldn't do a thing. I sat down on a tombstone and had a hemorrhage. I lost the baby there, on that tombstone. I'm convinced that I had a miscarriage because of Alain Soral and the anti-Semitic horrors he was spouting. Even if *Perfect Love* is mostly the Belfort story, I brought it back to myself, I put my private life in it. I wanted Soral to tell the story of leaving Formentera, which is engraved in my memory. I may hate him, but I experienced that moment as a good cinematic scene.

You would expect that filmmakers would film what they love, what they want to see, but here you filmed someone you hate. It's a beautiful gesture.

It's pretty perverse. But this guy is so weak, he wanted to make movies so much, that he didn't understand that I was using him, and that I hated him. He only understood that he was betraying Stéphane. The total betrayal of a friend, that amused me. But he does have one good quality, his use of language. He speaks very, very well, he's an orator with a relationship to words that I appreciate. Otherwise I wouldn't have sent him the scene. I handed the pages out to him as we were shooting and said to him, "You know it, right? You don't need to learn it." Like all great talkers, he's someone who only ever repeats himself in a loop—me too, probably, I just don't realize it.

As expected, he knew the text perfectly, nearly down to the comma. The crew and I were dying laughing, but he was amazing without understanding that I was using him. People are ready to do anything to act in a film. For *Dirty like an Angel*, I needed a gangster, an actor that looked like *M*,[20] with a slightly lunar face, like Claude-Jean Philippe,[21] who, by the way, didn't like me at all and hated my films. My assistant called him behind my back and, bizarrely, he jumped at the chance. It's unbelievable, people's desire to be in films. You ask someone to act in a film, and he doesn't say no, even if it means betraying his best friend or dropping his pants. After all, Claude-Jean Philippe played a corpse in pajamas in the film, literally full of shit, because after death you defecate, you empty yourself. And he did it. People want to see themselves, they want to make films.

You said that Perfect Love *is very autobiographical. The husband who no longer wants to sleep with you?*

Let's say a husband who doesn't have much libido. My children criticize me for the autobiographical aspect of my films a lot. But I have an alibi, it's a true story! I wanted language to be central, so I changed the social class so that the characters could be really verbal. I used the class milieu of my son's father rather than the actual social milieu of the murderer and his victim. He, by the way, is the same partner who inspired Paul in *Romance*, except that I treated that story in a mythic way, whereas *Perfect Love* is very realistic. Except for the ending, which is very expressionistic, when the camera is in the victim's place in a low-angle shot, and you can see the young man murdering her laughter.

How did you figure out the mise-en-scène of the murder? You do an abrupt shot/countershot that makes the scene very abstract, and the violence (the sodomy, the murder) stays off-screen.

---

20. A reference to Fritz Lang's film, which starred Peter Lorre (1931).
21. Film critic, writer, director, and television producer.

The brutality of emergency is always the thing that makes me figure out, the night before, how to shoot the next day's scene that seems totally unfilmable. In extremis, I'll find an extremely radical idea. As long as I had a very precise reenactment at the beginning, the sodomy could stay off-screen. Until the end, I said to Isabelle Renauld, "It's still a love scene, full of rage, absolutely, but he's not thinking about killing you. It's not until the last moment, when he notices the knife and you don't stop laughing, that he becomes a murderer, not before." That's the Belfort story. Two lovers who can neither break up nor live together. So he kills her for mocking him one too many times. You know that it's going to happen, and until the last moment, you don't understand how it's possible, because it's a love story. Up until the very last moment, then, it has to be a love story.

I delayed the turning point relentlessly. Then when it came, I filmed through the victim's eyes: her gaze became the camera. That's my grand theory of the subjective camera, and I have to fight everyone to impose it. Everyone gets upset and says, "You need an 'over-the-shoulder' shot," but I can't stand those. I reproduce my own gaze, which is the camera's. It's always about avoiding mediocre realism to get to the truth of the scene. I always oppose reality, which is factual, to truth, which is mythic. The idea was also that the viewer would take the fifty stab wounds, that they would be in the victim's place and see her handsome murderer.

Like Hitchcock?

I hadn't thought about Hitchcock, I was thinking Japanese. I was also thinking about Gide's writings, where he followed and reported on numerous trials. He mentions a concierge, a witness to a crime, who said that the man had struck his victim with fifty stab wounds like "a postal employee stamping mail." Obviously, the judges and jury thought the man had displayed a kind of fury that further exacerbated the crime. But Gide didn't think that stabbing someone fifty times makes you more guilty than stabbing them once! The number of stab wounds has nothing to do with it, and the opposite may even be true. Fifty stab wounds, that implies a loss of consciousness, while one or two is much more considered. With fifty, it's delirious, a trance, you're murdering something other than the body.

What, ultimately, did you want to film?

The idea that each of them was chosen by and attracted to the other because they were similar; they had the same flaws, so they weren't able to help each other surmount them. When he kills her, it's no longer possible for them to live together, but they can't live without each other either. To kill a woman, you have to love her: otherwise you divorce, you separate, which is much simpler. There, it's a matter of romantic alienation. You think that you're going to die without that person, but you can't live together because it's hell. If you kill her, the reason for the hell disappears.

Today, Perfect Love *tells the story of a femicide.*

Yes, of course, but for me it's above all a story of passionate love that rapidly degenerates. And I think that mine is a very precise description of a classic scene. When the woman doubts the virility of the man, he suddenly has to kill her—as Jonathann Daval did. There's no premeditation, only urgency. I'm not supporting or minimizing the murder of women. I think it's great that we can finally stop calling them "crimes of passion."

But you just said that someone could kill out of passion.

No, a person kills because he loves in an all-devouring way: the other devours you and you devour the other. In fact, you almost never really love the person—you understand that once the love is over. When you really analyze it, the power of the amorous myth is the thing that kills. They say that feelings take hold of us, that we fall prey to our emotions: nothing could be further from the truth, and that's not why they have the slightest objective consistency. When I take stock of my loves and passions, it's laughable. But how I believed in them, and how I suffered! And that was really useful for my work. I tell the stories that I told myself. That romantic phantasmagoria is primordial, it makes for great works of art, we pursue it our whole lives, but it's only a phantasmagoria. It's also cultural, and that's the subject of *Romance*.

In that phantasmagoria, men see us as their possessions. Even when you're no longer together, they can't stand it when you go with another man. Even when they're the ones leaving you because you've gotten ugly or too old. If you get together with someone else, someone younger or richer, they can't handle it. They own you until the end of time. When I was younger, I got very friendly with my exes, and we could console each other over temporary heartbreaks by sleeping together again … And then I decided there was no point; exes are exes. I only stay close with my children's fathers out of necessity. There's no point in seeing exes again and becoming friends. It's kind of a cursed friendship, a so-called friendship—they're always jealous, in reality. They don't like it when you succeed, they aren't supportive.

Do you think a kind of sexual or romantic domination exists that could be healthy? Healthier than another?

As the Marquise de Flers says in *The Last Mistress*: "The first to love has lost." A romantic relationship is never fair; the one who becomes enthralled by the other is the one who is going to suffer, whether it be the man or the woman. Afterward, the men can avenge themselves by beating us or killing us. But apart from that, you can't codify the amorous relationship, it's much more informal than that. First of all, falling in love isn't rational. Idealizing someone isn't a normal emotion, it makes no sense. And yet the fantasy takes over reality completely. We've all dreamed about it, falling in love. At first it's paradise, then one day it becomes hell. It's Shakespeare, "O Romeo, Romeo, wherefore art thou Romeo?" How do you answer such a stupid, inane, cartoonish question? And yet it's Shakespeare; and yet it's our life.

So it's impossible to have equality in love?

Desire is the back-and-forth between desire and nondesire, wanting and not wanting. That's desire. If you're equals, you're not making love. It's the back-and-forth between the weaker and the stronger one. You take turns becoming the weaker and the stronger one. That's what you have to understand, you move from one to the other. That's what I understood in the long-shot sequence in *Romance*, when Rocco starts to come as if he were dying of love, giving up power entirely. Total surrender of the magnificent, primordial stud. How do you expect men to get hard if there's no law of the strongest? It's in their genes. And suddenly, a power reversal. I've seen it with my own eyes, otherwise I would have never thought of it. Sex is full of many things, it's protean, it's incredible.

Is it because of the back-and-forth of desire that you make the camera movements you do in Perfect Love? *You move continuously from the man to the woman, like Ping-Pong. I don't remember if it's a tracking shot or a panning shot.*

Both, there's a circular tracking shot and a pan. And it's funny, because when they're talking on the beach, the camera lands on a Ping-Pong ball that's split in two. I didn't want to do a shot/countershot, since for me that always signifies opposition. But in life, it's different. In life, we're connected, bodies are connected in space. When I talk to you, I look you in the eyes, there's a relationship: somewhere, you enter into me, like the camera. We're connected here, you can feel it, it's not you *there* and me *here*. Speaking is a gift to the other, and you listen. Space is connected. In *Perfect Love*, I connected space.

I recently bought Le livre du plaisir *(The book of pleasure),*[22] *your anthology of pornographic literature that opens with a phrase from the Roman emperor Septimius: "He who writes sodomizes; he who reads is sodomized." What does that mean to you?*

In fiction, you capture the other, the actor, but also the spectator. There's no shot/countershot, the performance and then the spectator on the other side, peacefully sitting in his chair. No: he's there, between the camera and the actor, and his intimacy is involved. I undo the *gentleman's agreement*. That's probably what tends to make the spectator aggressive, because he isn't prepared to see himself up close. Incidentally, I love that book.

22. Catherine Breillat, ed., *Le livre du plaisir* (Éditions 1, 1999).

At first the editor wanted me to do an anthology of smutty garter-belt literature that I absolutely abhor.

You write this sentence in the introduction: "Literature is the most expansive and inoffensive experimental field in the world." Would you say the same thing about cinema?

No, because cinema is totalitarian. Literature is twenty-six letters of the alphabet that offer the world. In cinema, the image is what's captivating. Right now, I'm relishing looking at my son … uh, my film [*mon fils … mon film*], and I can clearly see that I'm devouring, that I can manipulate emotions, and that it isn't harmless for the spectator. You can make him believe in whatever you want: that there has been a murder, a rape …

You published a novel, Bad Love,[23] *that you wanted to adapt into a film starring Naomi Campbell and Christophe Rocancourt. It was, essentially, a remake of* Perfect Love.

But it was different, the man was different, much more carnal and rural. Naomi Campbell played a star who would have been ashamed if her relationship with that kind of guy became public. He wasn't really handsome, sort of boorish in body and mind. But he held out and made her go to his house, which was cramped and uncomfortable. The fact that she accepted was a form of domination. All they did was make love, physical love that became love full stop. The details were very different from *Perfect Love*. And maybe closer to *In the Realm of the Senses* (Nagisa Ōshima, 1976)

---

23. Catherine Breillat, *Bad Love* (Éditions Léo Scheer, 2007).

When you set out to shoot a remake of your own films, is it driven by a sense of dissatisfaction? Do you say, "I need to further, I could do more"?

No, I say to myself that I'm excavating inexhaustible subjects, so you can always have another version, cut another groove, but always on the same subject. It's not that I'm trying to go further to transgress even more, because deep down I never realize that I'm transgressing. There's an innocence about me when it comes to scandal.

What scene in Bad Love *did you want to film?*

The one that almost made me cry in *The Woman and the Puppet* (1898), Pierre Louÿs's novel, when he starts to beat his lover. When I wrote the screenplay, Marie Trintignant had been killed, and it became impossible to make the film: my heroine let herself be slaughtered, while taunting the guy, while saying it didn't even hurt. She was madly in love with this beast, but she was ashamed of it. This wasn't a publicized love affair, it was her secret. I know that it's possible to love a beast, it's happened to me. But that guy had an almost hallucinatory sense of carnal love that I never experienced again. A relationship to physical love that was really about love. Which is astonishing for someone like me, who has always lived with her fists clenched. Never relaxed. When they see me, chiropractors and masseurs tear their hair out, because that's the way I live, all tensed up. Christine Pascal was like that, Léa Drucker in *Last Summer*, I filmed her like that. I know I can't unclench my fists in life. Curiously enough, babies clench their fists, too.

BODY/HEAD

Romance • walking around with your sex between your legs • sex is thinking, fiction in motion • a filmmaker only ever films her gaze • transparent and pure as a crystal sword • not a single shadow on her face • you have no right to be there • it's much more important to be kissed than penetrated • Rocco surrenders • King Kong looking at the tiny woman in his hand • I can't be anything other than a manipulator • you have to sleep with the bull • directors manipulate • the denial of the husband who doesn't want to see • *Romance* is against all of that: sex or no sex • the *baby blues* • an actor never simulates anything • the return-to-reality coach • you enter into a film as if you were entering into Carmel

Murielle Joudet: Romance *is a project that you thought about for a long time.*

Catherine Breillat: Yes, I had wanted to make it for twenty years, the screenplay fascinated everyone who read it, but it was impossible to do it then. Until all of a sudden, it was in the air: Lars von Trier, Bertolucci, and other renowned directors all wanted to make films that included nonsimulated sex acts. I decided that that approach had been mine for far too long not to take the initiative. The moment had arrived. I had gotten an advance on the receipts for *The Last Mistress*, and I gave that up to make *Romance*. Miraculously, I was able to secure financing, along with support from ARTE, for a screenplay that was thoroughly pornographic, but if the film were rated X, we would have been forced to give back all of the funding. Jean-François Lepetit, my producer, took this enormous risk. Of course, I was afraid and I said to my actress, Caroline Ducey, that we shouldn't have any prejudices, because what makes a film obscene is the fear of being obscene. If you're reluctant because you're afraid, then the reluctance reads as obscenity. Ōshima went through the same struggle, he describes it in his journal. He gave me the courage to trust it.

What did you want to show, to say?

We're all walking around with our sex between our legs—we simply pretend to ignore it. You can't escape sex, it's everywhere. Except that sexual acts have never been filmed other than as a show of flesh, without ever giving the act any meaning. But when you sleep with someone, it's always a search: it could be depravity, denigration, simple pleasure, or even unconditional love. It's thinking, fiction in motion. And the hallmark of porn films is the absence of fiction. What's thrown at us in close-up is just a degrading display of slimy flesh, simply to prove how disgusting women's sexes are, and, conveniently, they don't ever come. It goes in and out, like the needle of a sewing machine. The man penetrates the woman and because of that fact alone, he is superior to her. That he's the one to fill the hole is enough to satisfy his pride. That revolts me because when I make love, I'm sure that I'm not like that.

It's about reconnecting sex to its fictional role.

Yes, and that requires making a film without any censorship at all, where none of the sex acts are simulated, and my gaze as a filmmaker transfigures all of it. Because deep down, a filmmaker only ever films her gaze. Why is it that when I film two people having tea, that's cinema, but if I film a sexual act, then the shot can only be pornographically vulgar? Saying that means you think of yourself as a filmmaker who's unable to put your own stamp on what you're filming. I asked Godard to play the character of François Berléand, thinking that I needed a filmmaker for those scenes. He wrote me a rejection letter that quoted Truffaut, who had theorized that you can't film actual physical acts and still call it cinema. That's low self-esteem. Everything I'm not allowed to film, I film.

It must have been very complicated to find an actress who was able to accept the challenge of nonsimulated scenes.

The question of whether or not the actress we chose would accept the rawness of the script came later. During casting, we had to stoically ignore it. I saw nearly two hundred actresses improvise and I constructed a *shortlist* of fifteen whom I wanted to see read lines. I ultimately kept only two: Laure Marsac and Caroline Ducey. The one who accepted the explicit nature of the film would be the right one. Laure Marsac wrote me a very sweet little letter to explain that she loved the screenplay but couldn't bring herself to do nonsimulated scenes. So I chose Caroline, who accepted the premise of the film. She had already acted in a film by Cédric Kahn, *Too Much Happiness* (1994); at the time she was named Caroline Trousselard. I told her, "You can't have that last name and make this film, you'll be a laughing stock! You have to change your name." She did it, even though she was really attached to her original surname.

So everything was spelled out in Caroline Ducey's contract?

Of course not, but it's very explicit in the screenplay, which was attached to the contract. None of my intentions were hidden. It was also announced everywhere in the press. Caroline agreed to make the film with full knowledge of the facts. She assured me that she would do all of the explicitly written scenes, but she didn't want to tell her agent. Naturally, there was the risk that at the last moment she would refuse to play certain scenes. Even if you marry someone, if you don't want to sleep with him anymore, that's your right. To ignore that means rape.

But Caroline was totally loyal, and determined, believing as much as I did in the necessity of this film that, more than any other, followed the dangerous path of every heroic quest. She was as transparent and pure as that legendary crystal sword. I respected her and loved her madly. She moved me deeply every time that I filmed her. I made sure at every moment that she wouldn't be debased or degraded by the sexual acts she was going to engage in.

I called her Joan of Arc and I was determined to film her like a saint. I said to Yorgos Arvanitis (the director of photography): "Above all, not a single shadow on her face!" Nothing! I had to protect her image from any idea of taint or indecency at all costs. That kind of lighting work leaves no place for the idea of "happening" or improvisation: it requires absolute precision of movements, of actors, of the camera. Nothing should be left to chance.

No shadow, apart from that little strand of hair that falls on her face.

I always put in that strand! Incidentally, Samuel Kircher has it in *Last Summer*, too, but that just happened by chance. In *36 fillette*, Delphine Zentout's hair is in her eyes. I always undo a strand, wet it with my saliva, and then place it, like in a Japanese print. It makes the face much more graphic. And then it's also yin and yang, like a hairline crack.

She agreed to act in every scene?

Yes, yes, yes. For the fellatio scene, Sagamore Stévenin was so happy, you know how men always brag, "Oh, that's no problem for me, I'm really big when I get hard!" He went off to discreetly jerk himself off but as soon as he got back to the set, he lost his erection almost completely. I would have liked for him to be just even a little bit more hard, right when Marie says that his sex is like a pulsating bird, but it just wasn't working. Caroline unhesitatingly took him in her mouth and delivered the dialogue beautifully. Every sex scene works with a very tightly written text block.

In interviews done in the years after the shoot, Caroline Ducey has said that she wasn't warned about the brutality of certain scenes, and that she was the victim of a rape. I'd like to go over the two disputed scenes in detail. The first concerns the long take with Rocco Siffredi that ends, if I understand correctly, in nonsimulated intercourse. What happened during the shooting of that take?

It was a very long and meticulous feat of engineering, setting up a tracking shot that lasts eight and a half minutes. After a four-minute monologue, they had to have sex. Understand that in filmmaking, you usually shoot three and a half minutes of useful footage a day, on average. It was an arduous task. Rocco had no idea what a "normal" shoot was like, and we had no idea what a porn shoot was like. He didn't want anyone to see him go limp—he ended up offering that to me in *Anatomy of Hell.*

On a porn shoot, you do your scene and that's it. But for this, he dutifully jerked off for three hours for nothing. Yorgos and his camera crew wanted to leave the set; his wife was the one who convinced him to stay, saying that *Romance* was a very important film. The sound engineer shouted that it wasn't cinema. Caroline complained, "There's no love there, he isn't looking me in the eyes." It was six hours before we could even start shooting. The atmosphere was so negative, the contempt that was leveled at Rocco was so violent, that he snapped and ended up leaving the set. And we were only doing the technical rehearsals! I rushed toward him. I can still see him turning around and, with his pride deeply wounded, saying to me, "You can think whatever you want about me, Catherine, but I've never made love to a woman who didn't want me." I answered, "Caroline doesn't want you, she will never want you. It's Marie, the character, who is going to sleep with you." I added that I didn't want to make the 365th porn film of Rocco Siffredi, that didn't interest me. What I wanted was … I didn't know what I wanted. I wanted something that had never been filmed before. Something so totally intimate that you had no right to be there. He said, "Oh, I see, you want the real Rocco, the way I am with my wife." I answered yes, and that there would be fourteen takes, because we weren't in a porn film and the acting was the most important thing of all.

And what did you say to Caroline Ducey?

Rocco complained that Caroline didn't want him. Caroline complained that Rocco didn't love her. It was desire versus emotion. We never escape it. I went to find Caroline and told her that we would at least get the dialogue in the can, that I'd cut very quickly if it wasn't perfect. If I let the scene go, it was up to her to decide if she had sex with Rocco or not. Of course, that's what I wanted, but it was her decision … I had to explain to her again that with him, it was specifically not a romance: "He's a friend/lover, someone you can get off with, freely, without taboos or prejudices, it's a lot of fun, but you don't love him and he doesn't love you." Even if there's some ambiguity at the end because Marie says that she never kisses and ends up doing so. When someone makes love to you that well, you can't resist. It's much more important to be kissed than penetrated, and I would love for girls to have that philosophy, which is much more gratifying in the end, and means that we don't have to feel ashamed just because we gave in to someone a hundred years ago.

So did you do fourteen takes of that shot?

Yes, but only the long monologue, I cut before the sex. It had to be flawless, sublime. You absolutely can't not have ethics when you do that kind of scene. Simulated or not. So we started shooting. Never in my life has my throat been so dry and tight. Caroline had this four-minute monologue and I was thinking, "Is this good enough? Should I interrupt her?" We did fourteen takes, then I let the scene roll.

Until the nonsimulated sex, then?

Then they had sex for the first time. It was very beautiful and very raw. I could have been satisfied with that. That take was probably more commercial than the one I chose. "You're not just a first-take actress; now that it's done, it's not so bad! Why don't we try to do another one?" She agreed. We asked Yorgos to put the camera back on the rails and we did another take. And then what happened on the second take was totally different, it was incredibly gentle: Rocco surrendered, he wasn't a stud anymore. It was like a power exchange: the law of the jungle in reverse. The weaker became the stronger and vice versa. He surrendered when he orgasmed with this incredible moan, it was plaintive and ecstatic. I considered that to be the meaning of the film: the man becoming the weaker one. The power that circulates on the woman's side while the biggest stud in the world slowly dies. Like King Kong looking at the tiny woman in his hand. That obviously was the magical take.

The next day, there were lots of scenes planned, totally pornographic, of a liberated girl getting off with her lover. I watched the two takes all night, I thought that I had achieved a sublime moment that only worked as a culmination. We couldn't just move on to porn scenes on the pretext that we were making a film with real sex in it. I questioned for a long time whether or not that was a lack of courage on my part. But no: with that scene, I had found the meaning of the film. I canceled the following scenes and let Rocco go. He left a day early, without asking for the rest of his pay. For him, that scene was the hardest he had ever experienced on a set.

But when you see the scene, you can't tell if the act was simulated or not.

I wasn't going to move them or make then spread their legs so there wouldn't be any ambiguity and everyone would definitely know. I didn't want for the sex to be totally disconnected from the person—that's what porn films do. I actually made *Anatomy of Hell* because I thought I had lost my nerve on *Romance*, particularly when Marie says, "I can't stand the proximity of my face and my pussy." Except that you don't see the pussy: I bailed, I didn't have the nerve to shoot it, even though that's what was written. It was incredibly hard to do, hard to think that you're still making art, when you're filming the same thing as porn. That's probably why I pared that film down way too much. I didn't want anything to be able to reach or tarnish Caroline, or for anything to prevent her from having a career. Nothing ever prevented her.

She blames you for having hidden the identity of her partner until the day of the shoot. Why do that?

I hid it from everyone. I was extremely worried that there would be advance buzz about the film, that they'd say in the press that I was about to make a porn film with Rocco Siffredi. And plus, I chose him at the last minute. I had been looking for him everywhere and finally he showed up. He called the office barely an hour before the actor originally planned to play the part was supposed to sign the contract. He was enthusiastic, ready to book his own plane tickets—he didn't know that in cinema, they take care of everything.

Why did you want him in particular?

Because I loved him. I saw him on a Guillaume Durand show with Phillipe Sollers where they talked about eroticism and pornography, and Rocco was the only one who spoke with a kind of freedom and specificity that I'd never heard before. I had seen some of his porn films, that way he has of undulating like a wave: he was the only one really making love. The first time I met him face-to-face, he plunged his eyes into mine in such a sexual way that I had to use all my strength to counter him with an icy stare, otherwise I wouldn't be the director any more. He wanted to determine if he was having an effect and, of course, he was having a strong effect. It's very hard to indicate to him that you don't want him, that you don't want to sleep with him. He penetrates you with his eyes.

And after the film is over, are you allowed to sleep together?

Yes. Except that after the shoot we had become friends, and once you're friends, you don't want to sleep together anymore. But I never sleep with my actors. I sleep with the film. The toreador in Luis Miguel Dominguin's book says something that I quote all the time. In his autobiography, he says, "In bullfighting season, you mustn't have any love affairs, because the bull can smell it, and that's the cornada. In bullfighting season, you have to sleep with the bull."

Caroline Ducey said that you took advantage of her innocence. Were you aware that she was young and therefore malleable?

She was only twenty-two, of course, but she was very much an adult, and she wasn't as fainthearted as she would have you believe now, because our era has experienced a fundamental shift. Directors manipulate—what else do you want them to do? I'm a director, I can't be anything other than a manipulator. Otherwise the actors would perform their scenes by themselves, and I'd stay home. After the fact, she can obviously regret it and think that she was too young. I think that you can be naive at any age. I was, even when I was seventy.

Let's move on to the rape scene that is truly a black hole in Romance, *straddling fantasy and nightmare. Here is a quote from the* IndieWire *article published during the retrospective of your films in New York, in which Caroline Ducey was interviewed: "When they shot the rape scene that arrives late in the movie, Ducey alleges that Breillat told the male actor—a non-professional man cast shortly beforehand—to actually try to penetrate the actress on camera. 'Catherine asked me to take my pants off like five minutes before we were rolling,' Ducey said in a phone interview this week. 'I was getting ready to act. I didn't think it could happen for real. This guy, I was about to kill him.' Ducey said she pushed him off and Breillat stopped rolling; they completed the scene, with no penetration, in the second take. That's the one in the movie. 'I was really angry at Catherine, because she didn't need to organize the scene like that at all,' Ducey said. 'It was not a snuff movie. But I still respect it, because I know what I put into it, so I don't want to throw it all in the trash. I think the movie is important, and Catherine is a real director.'"*

First of all, I didn't ask her to take her pants off for the simple reason that she was wearing the white muslin-wool dress that I designed for the film. Second, in the screenplay it's scene 39, it's written very explicitly that nothing should be simulated, it's indicated in the text. I luckily was able to find the shooting script and prove that Caroline was lying on that point. Without that, my career in the United States would have been finished, that's what she wanted. It's clearly the goal she's been pursuing for twenty years.

Anyway, if memory serves, the rape scene was shot on the last studio day. Around six feet away from Caroline, a porn actress was trying to get an erection out of the actor. Six feet farther away was Yorgos Arvanitis, his puller, and the grips who were getting ready to shoot. I was right there, with the assistant monitor operator, the script supervisor, and my first assistant. We all had headsets, we didn't miss a single word that Caroline said: it would have been impossible for a rape to take place under those conditions without the active complicity of all those people.

It's my understanding that things went badly with the actor who had to play the rape scene with Caroline Ducey?

That's right, he turned out to be somewhat identical to the role, except that he couldn't get it up and, every time, Caroline was inwardly jubilant: she triumphed over him. She was proud, very cute, she didn't refuse to do the scene but she was probably very happy that we couldn't do it. After five or six turns around this merry-go-round where he couldn't manage to get hard, I decided, "Oh well, the scene will be simulated." I must have said, "OK, fine, I don't care, just stick to her completely so we can't see that you're not hard and we'll do the scene like that, simulated." The tension that dominated the set, certainly the anxiety that

Caroline felt about doing it, and the absolutely brilliant actress she was at the time, all of that made the scene staggering and certainly more violent than if they had actually performed the act. It was an extraordinary scene, an absolutely sublime shot.

Even though it's simulated and acted, that scene is brutal, especially when the actor turns out to be a dirtbag.

Even when it's simulated and acted, every scene should give the illusion of truth. That's the principle of cinema itself. Would you have liked for me to soften the scene to shut my detractors up? The rape in that scene is brutal and violent because Caroline is a masterful actress who stunned us all. Period. The actor, clearly humiliated by not being able to get hard, then burst into Caroline's dressing room and insulted her pretty much the way he does on-screen, he was very vulgar. I unceremoniously threw him out. That explains some of it. Still, after that scene we were all beaming. My producer found us by the lake at the hotel, drinking white wine, laughing, having fun— and of course, Caroline was there. In short, not the atmosphere that there would have been after a real rape. Furthermore, she kept saying how the shoot was "pure joy." And to *Technikart*, she said: "I came out of the film unscathed, although there were two tense moments: the scene with Rocco, and the seduction scene with Berléand." It's absolutely true. If she doesn't mention the rape scene, it's because there was no need to.

Why did the fact that the actor was Iranian matter so much?

When she was hired on *Romance*, Caroline told me that she wanted to break up with her boyfriend and that the film would give her a definitive opportunity. Since he was Iranian and macho, he wouldn't have stayed with a girl who did that. In fact, she broke up with her boyfriend and got back together with him after the shoot. When the edit came out, she came to see me, very worried, telling me what would happen if her boyfriend Pedram found out that she had sex with Rocco Siffredi. I told Caroline that I had used the second take, which was much less raw, so she could tell her boyfriend that she hadn't had sex with Rocco because you can't really tell. We organized a screening for Pedram and his only comment was, "Oh, she didn't have sex with Rocco!" Jean-François, my assistant, and I were floored; he was a cuckold who completely denied the subject of the film—it's funny, because *Last Summer* has the same subject, the denial of the husband who doesn't want to see anything, know anything. But afterward, how do you live in the lie? That type of secret is very heavy to carry. I doubt that, for Caroline, that lie had no consequences for her and her relationship.

So that lie was arranged, but I warned her: the last thing she needed was to have to answer to journalists asking her if she had really slept with him or not. I told her to say, "So what? What's it to you? It's cinema. You believe in what you see." It wasn't up to her to issue a certificate of good behavior when *Romance* is against all of that: sex or no sex, it doesn't matter. It doesn't take anything away from you. Still, I never should have arranged that lie.

So she's always denied having had sex with Rocco Siffredi?

Yes, and when I saw her again in 2006, I was astonished to realize that she had convinced herself of her own lie.

You gave her a small role in The Last Mistress *in 2007.*

After my stroke, I wanted to bring together all of the actresses who have been important to me, in *The Last Mistress*. She told me that she wasn't doing well and I was honestly sorry, I was very troubled by the state she was in. She talked to me and I realized, stupefied, that she had supposedly forgotten (I don't know if she was acting in good faith or if she forgot) having slept with Rocco Siffredi. Let's say that she forgot: she knows deep down that something sexual happened. So she shifted it to the sex happening during the rape scene, and not with Rocco Siffredi. I'm not a psychiatrist, I can't explain with any certainty what could have been a kind of traumatic transfer and amnesia of the actual sex scene. I think that through denying to everyone that she had slept with Rocco, she got entangled in her lie and ended up believing it. She wanted me to give her Asia [Argento's] role in *The Last Mistress*, she begged me desperately. But what can I do? Just because I work with one actress doesn't mean that I have to have her act in all of my films. I know that she blamed and blames me to no end, but she was poles apart from the role, and I didn't owe her anything. Especially not sacrificing the film of my *renaissance*. She accepted the minor role, gracefully and happily, it seemed. At the time, I thought she was sincere, but now, I've seen her lie too much, change versions of her story while expecting me to give her another role.

Did you see her again after that?

I saw her again in August 2011, after I had written *Abuse of Weakness*. I was deeply alone, weakened, desperate. Six months later, I received this letter, very well crafted and extremely disarming. You'd have to have a heart of stone not to be moved by it, even if it was all a lie. She claimed that she had been sexually abused by the Iranian actor. The letter ended strangely: "As I told you, I read your book *Abuse of Weakness*, which I thought was brilliant, and then I thought that daring to work with you again might perhaps repair things. I don't know." The reparation was Isabelle Huppert's role, no more, no less: she demanded it as bitterly as when she had demanded making *The Last Mistress*, as if she were owed it.

In an interview given to Nouvel Obs *in 2014, she recalled a traumatic experience that, this time, concerned the scene with Rocco Siffredi, but when the journalist asked her if the scene was simulated, she answered, "Of course it was! Well, that's my point of view … If you ask Rocco that question, he'll tell you that it wasn't simulated …"*[24]

Caroline constantly fluctuated. I never know what to expect from her. In a bonus feature from 2019 on the American Blu-ray of *Romance*, she claims to have had a double for all of the sex scenes—which is obviously false. She's used every possibly means to find an angle of attack. I'm not talking about the rumors that get back to me from time to time, how Caroline wants my hide and wants to cancel my career. She wrote to Léa Drucker to warn her not to trust me. I learned that two years later, in 2021, she asked for a meeting at Cinémathèque to tell them that she had suffered a rape attempt at my instigation during the scene with Rocco Siffredi.

24. Caroline Ducey, "Caroline Ducey : 'Rocco Siffredi, je ne savais pas qui c'était,'" interview by Guillaume Loison, *Nouvel Obs*, November 29, 2014.

The only thing that seems coherent and perfectly understandable, in view of what I see in the film, is that the shoot for Romance *must have been completely harrowing for a young actress. And that she became aware of that violence later, once the enthusiasm had passed.*

The shoot was very exhilarating, very joyful, and I really think that it's the period after *Romance* in which everything started to turn. After the shoot, I dove into editing. I remember that everyone had a massive bout of the *blues*. Everyone is probably too connected to each other on a shoot, everyone loves each other, you see each other every day, you swear that you're going to see each other afterward and make another film, but that never happens. I don't know, but I think she must have experienced that. Returning to reality is brutal, it's a sort of *baby blues*. You return to a life that you no longer understand. Even when you go to Club Med for eight days, you're out of step with reality … For a film, you have to imagine that it's even more absorbing, that it's even worse. Nothing else matters and then suddenly it's over, and you can't enjoy anything anymore. You have to be surrounded, I guess. Samuel also had his *baby blues* after *Last Summer*, and his mother took care of him. Who took care of Caroline? Definitely not a guy she had to lie to.

After everything that she gave you on Romance*, she thought it was reasonable to ask for another role, another film. She had become your actress and it was probably very complicated to find roles after that film.*

I can't take care of Caroline. I make films from time to time; an actress has to make them all of the time. She couldn't bear that I work with other actresses, or the breakup that happened in

Rome. You have to understand that she experienced real harassment from journalists, they were constantly asking her if she had had sex with Rocco Siffredi. I know she confided in Frédéric Bonnaud because she said that he, at least when he was a journalist, never asked her if she had had sex with him or not. Which means that that harassment of questions, did she or didn't she, was very painful for her. Incidentally, Rocco is the one who became a star after *Romance*. Not her, or me.

You don't think Romance *might have prevented her from having a career?*

You can't say that after *Romance* she was a pariah, or devastated, or unable to work. She was so highly praised that even the negative reviews of the film lauded her performance. The head of the Norwegian censorship board, instead of banning the film, added an advisory for young girls. She had a starring role in a film with Melvil Poupaud, then with Jacques Doillon, who is not a minor director. *Romance* gave her a name. Then she had to do something with it. She had to say, "So what?" or what she said on Swiss television. They asked her what it was like to do nonsimulated scenes and she had this magnificent response: "An actor never simulates anything." I think that's amazing, and that she should have kept that perspective.

Would you say, given the project and the fact that it was the first time a film like that had been made in France, do you think that that shoot was a sort of unsupervised experiment?

A Real Young Girl was much "worse" than *Romance*, a hundred times worse, and there were no problems. You can't say, "Today, we'd do it like this"; that was twenty years ago. I think now with the proliferation of young amateur actors in cinema, we need to seriously reflect on what the work of a film actor is about, and its dangers. And we're not going to find the solution with self-proclaimed intimacy coaches and other hypocrisies like that. "Return-to-reality coaches" who help actors at the end of an overly intense shoot would be far more effective than these little ayatollahs who surf the waves of our current puritanism to justify unbearable interference and the *droit du regard*—hence censorship—over sex scenes in film. Let's just ban them, these sex scenes, if they're going to be controlled by these henchmen without any real qualifications whom directors now have to use to avoid exposing themselves to criticism and accusation.

Did you talk to her enough during the shoot?

Probably not. I never talk about roles with my actors. It's written down, you just have to read it. But Caroline is probably the actress I talked to the most. A film, the meaning of a film, is never frozen in marble. You don't understand the stakes of a scene until the moment you do it, not before. It's impossible to really prepare yourself. That anxiety that mounts before a shoot is normal and necessary for the beauty of the film. It's the proof that you place the bar very high and that you're aware that the stakes are high.

You have to understand something that isn't obvious when you haven't experienced it: everyone is under the influence on a shoot, the influence of the film that you have to finish, scene after scene. I often say that you enter into a film as if you were entering into Carmel. You only speak the words that belong to the film, your own words are forbidden. And if the emotions, the gestures, belong to the character, you have to really feel them. And it's up to me to get them to shed their skins on the shore of reality and reach the other shore of fiction. Because yes, cinema is carnivorous and cannibalistic. It isn't moral, but that's the way it is.

She undoubtedly threw herself body and soul into a shoot that was bound to be grueling. You tell yourself you'll hang on, but it's impossible to imagine the consequences.

Whenever you have a leading role, every shoot is demanding and psychically dangerous. You experience a maelstrom of successive emotions. And the rhythm of film doesn't allow for the time to reflect that theater does. You must necessarily throw yourself into it body and soul [*à corps perdu*]—what a beautiful and perfect expression. The actor who played Frankenstein's monster went mad afterward; it's never trivial, entering into a role. Actors make films with their flesh and blood, that's why they get paid the most. And afterward, it's very complicated to reintegrate who you are, especially when you make such an exhilarated and exhilarating film. You can never find that happiness again; you find yourself stuck in a drab, bleak life where you're bored stiff with "Did you sleep with Rocco Siffredi?" on a loop. Obviously, *Romance* is too intense and too dangerously innovative a film, it would be impossible to remake it today. Caroline perhaps paid the price for that and I regret it. But that doesn't explain or excuse the highly variable accusations that Caroline persists in making against me. She probably thinks, at a minimum, that I owe her another film. But that's not in my power: I don't make enough films for that. I'm only on my fourteenth; if I had made more, I would have written one for her. There are actresses who may think that I owe them something, but I can't give them anything.

SOLVE ET COAGULA

In the Realm of the Senses • passion as a test, pleasure as an anguish • colors act, you know • the great painters always save me—the purity that's demanded of us and that chills us • oh well, I'm Don Quixote • on the importance of being hated • a monochrome Mondrian • black or white magic • my heroines are rarely seeking the other • I like Natascha Kampusch • Rogozhin was my dream • I want to be able to be against a woman • when you're an artist, you want to be unique • better to destroy it all • I wanted to see how I was born • a sketch, a theory • actors aren't the color red

Murielle Joudet: *What do you find moving in* In the Realm of the Senses?

Catherine Breillat: The fact that he presents a vision of absolute love, reduced to the essential, the elementary: physical love, pure and simple. Pornography, for once, offers an image of holiness. It's like an initiatory journey with no way out. Those who embark on it experience passion as a test, pleasure as anguish. The anguish comes not from the fact that the physical act exists, we're shown it all on-screen—but from the fact that it doesn't actually exist. It doesn't exist beyond the moment the act is committed. Its fulfillment is like its death. *In the Realm of the Senses* isn't a "Japanese print" for me. It's a great film, and proof that it was time for me to confront a kind of intimate pornography that obviously has nothing to do with the films made by the porn industry.

Do you feel trapped by that subject?

It's not a trap because no one else is doing it. What's more, an auteur is always trapped in his style and his oeuvre. My oeuvre is coherent from beginning to end; I've never made a film that doesn't deal with it. Not one.

Why does Marie, the heroine of Romance, *never stop talking? That's also the case for all of your heroines …*

Because she says things about sex, identity, and sexual relationships that have never been verbalized before. It was long believed to be merely an obscene subject, even though it's a fundamental one. I had to hit the audience with truths they didn't dare admit to themselves. I tell them to their faces, on the big screen. And I have the luxury of not being rated X.

When we see couples who are somewhat settled down in your films, it becomes very creepy. In the domestic part of Romance, *everything is white, carceral, medical. They watch TV. It's deadly boring.*

That part happened very suddenly. I had a production designer who was trying to give me a psychological speech about the sets and my character. I can't stand that, I hate psychology. My films are a maelstrom of contradictory things that I have inside me and that appear in a radiant way on-screen. And at that point, I can't lie to myself anymore. During the film's preproduction, I went to see a Georges de La Tour exhibition. The first works that were sort of beige, "autumn leaves," didn't interest me at all. Then I got to the transcendent works, with that totally immaculate, transparent white, and those reds made from egg tempera that are absolutely sumptuous, nothing like a mediocre acrylic red at all. I was floored by the incredible whiteness of the skin, that transparency that gives the impression that you're looking at the soul. From a lighting point of view, what struck me was that famous hand where you can see the candle shining through it.[25] I wanted Caroline [Ducey] to have that incandescence, and to be able to see through her. The great painters always save me, and in the case of *Romance*, the Georges de La Tour exhibition changed everything. I fired the production designer and hired Frédérique Belvaux. I decided that the colors would be the alchemic colors of La Tour, the brown of the naked earth, the white of the Renaissance and the red of royalty,

---

25. Georges de La Tour's *The Education of the Virgin* (ca. 1650).

which singularly changed the film and gave it, along with a high level of visual sophistication, the look of an initiation quest. Colors act, you know.

How did you direct Caroline Ducey?

I don't direct actors, I enchant them, and vice versa. It's a symbiotic relationship. I chose Caroline because, ultimately, she was mine from the beginning, she belonged to my cinema. When she arrived at casting, she was wearing cheap little blue-rhinestone earrings, very mediocre, bad hair, a trapeze skirt. I could have overlooked her; to transform her into Marie, everything would have to be redone. But, how do I put this, as soon as I shot her in close-up, the relationship between the bottom of her brow bone and her lower eyelid was so pure, it was straight out of quattrocento. That's what I like. She acted incredibly well, her cheeks were full of emotion. It's a kind of instinct, a thunderbolt that often happens when I meet my actors. Then I take over, I dress them, I find them a hairstyle, I decide everything. Before, when I was able to do it, I did everything, I made up my actresses, I gave them a rose-pink foundation, very pale but pinkish—on film, you don't see the emotion when it's ivory. Emotion lives in pink, it's the flush of blood just under the skin. You have to fight against the habit of washing out all of the pink when you're calibrating color, because fashion photography only shows us bronzed bodies.

Do you also choose the sets?

For me the sets are part of the costumes: they envelop the actor. After the La Tour exhibition, I decided on the set decoration for

François Berléand's apartment. He was playing the role of a smuggler: he ties her up, but in truth he takes her to the other side of the masochistic temptation. There were some magical objects on set: a book of high magick, a very old edition, silver chandeliers in the form of a cobra, charged with oriental magic. There were treasures from Cambodian royalty, there was also a little chair from an African king, a taxidermied white cobra that symbolized the destruction of everything, all the forces of evil. The colors belonged to the hermetic tradition and to "l'Oeuvre au Noir."[26] And everything else, Caroline's and Sagamore's apartments, was white. Yorgos Arvanitis took me by the hand and said, "Catherine, this is impossible, I can't film this, you have to put at least a little tint in the white for it to go with white skin." I told him, "No, if everything is white, radically white, then it's something else." And in fact it chilled the actors, it "frigidified" them. There's no sex, everything's frigid. And yet there's a purity, a purity that is demanded of us and that chills us.

You film that like a nightmare of purity.

Yes, because that's not what purity is. Purity is the purity of seventeenth-century paintings. In *Last Summer*, I did the same thing, I opposed the two kinds of loves: reasonable love and ecstatic love, which is itself unbearable, even when it is bearable.

---

26. In alchemical treatises, the phrase *l'Oeuvre au Noir* (the Black Work) … refers to the phase of separation and dissolution of substance that was, they say, the most difficult part of the Great Work. It is still debated whether or not this expression applied to daring experiments on matter itself, or symbolically meant tests of the mind liberating itself from routine and prejudice. It undoubtedly meant both, alternately or simultaneously." Marguerite Yourcenar, *The Abyss* (London: Black Swan, 1976).

I fell madly in love with my husband, the father of my older daughter, and it lasted six years. Then, conjugality got the better of love. That's good too, that's reassuring: you have kids, it's good, you don't want to lose that, but at the same time, it's a funeral for the imagination, for poetry and freedom, that's the way it is. It's great, but still. Were we made to be alienated?

One senses, in Romance, *that life is only bearable in the circulation of those two worlds: the ideal and the concrete.*

I'm totally an idealist. I know it doesn't work, but I think you have to follow your ideal; you can achieve it but you can't hold on to it. Still, it's wonderful always to be idealistic, even though it's pointless. Oh, well, I'm Don Quixote. When I make films, I'm an idealist. If I were practical, I would have had much more success. The idealist has the advantage of exaltation, that gives life meaning, even if the feeling is as brief and fleeting as life itself. That's what I want, anyway.

What are the disadvantages of being an idealist?

People hate you, they don't understand you. I wrote an article in the film review *Trafic*, "De l'importance d'être haï" (On the importance of being hated),[27] but no matter how much you theorize it, it's still very difficult to bear. Even if writing about it is cathartic, you realize that yes, if you want to do important things, you're going to be hated. People want to kill you, but they'll end up adopting you. Anything that's important disturbs

---

27. Catherine Breillat, "De l'importance d'être haï," *Trafic*, no. 50 (May 2004): 109–16.

things, and when you disturb things, you're hated. The ones who cash out are the ones who do the same thing as you, but after you, once you've opened the breach.

Why does your heroine cry when she's tied up?

Because it's unbearable. Did you see how I tied her up? She was bound, a ball in her mouth, with the gag like a third eye over it: you feel like you're suffocating inside, you bear it until it becomes unbearable. I finally told François Berléand to tie her up in silence, although there was dialogue planned. In the end it's Marie talking in her in her head, while he meticulously applies himself to drawing the lines of power. It's a ritual. For that, I had to make a sort of monochrome Mondrian with the cord. In the end, maybe I'm only ever filming moving paintings.

It was especially important that Berléand didn't fumble any of his gestures. The painter's stroke is precise. It's a line that goes straight to the point, like an arrow. I wanted a cere-monial masochist with this whole seductive side, I thought a lot about Monteiro in that instance, about *God's Comedy* (1995). I said to Yorgos, "You know, we have to shoot right now, I don't know what's going to happen, but we have to shoot whatever happens." After Berléand tied up Caroline, he had to fall adoringly at her feet. And then, he really got some-where through that manic, poetic, intransigent idealism. When Berléand lifted Caroline's body over the chair, she was weightless. It was hallucinatory, it looked like she weighed nothing at all. I was shocked, and collapsed behind my big scarf; I cried because it was so magical. Whether it was white magic or black magic, I don't know. It contained all of the symbolism of "solve et coagula."[28] We did the scene a second time but the miracle never happened again, we could feel the weight of it, it screwed everything up.

It's unbearable to be tied up like that, but that's what the heroine has to experience. Those are the trials of the quest for the Holy Grail: she has to follow the dangerous path, walk the razor's edge, because that's the way it has to be, she has to survive all of the tests. And when Robert finally removes the gag, she sobs and laughs like a grieving child. Who knows where that incredible sorrow comes from—those sobs that are like agony, uncontrollable. Nothing like the tears of a César-winning actress. We shot that scene many times because Caroline cried very easily but had a hard time making it come from her belly. She was in pain, but at the same time, she said it was fine and that he didn't have to tie her up less tightly. Then Caroline managed to get herself in that insane state, she started to laugh and cry with her whole soul. Berléand was so overwhelmed that he didn't know what to do and patted her on the head. That was obviously the magical take.

What was your heroine seeking?

Herself. My heroines are rarely seeking the other.

Your films could be misunderstood as being about a right to pleasure or the female orgasm, although they're never about that. They're identity quests.

---

28. "Dissolve and coagulate," an alchemical formula that consists of decomposing a substance and its base elements before transforming it into something new.

I never make films about the orgasm or about pleasure, I don't care about that. That's not what counts. There's something more important. I'm searching for ecstasy, the transparent body, that state of nearly immobile ecstasy where you escape all material contingency. Penetration, sex, doesn't interest me except as a means to realize the transparent body. Of course, it has to move through that, but what interests me is the passage from the trivial to the divine, that sensation of eternity. That happens very rarely and when it doesn't happen, we shouldn't deprive ourselves of the orgasm and pleasure. I couldn't agree more.

I feel that it's important that we specify that that isn't your subject.

That isn't my cinema at all. My cinema is about ritual. Idealism is ritual, we're dealing with symbols of purity, divinity. Caroline is Joan of Arc, a saint on a crusade. Sexuality is simply the path to amorous abstraction. The path is sexual, that's the way it is. But because we've turned it into a commercial, obscene object, we tend to forget that. I don't know what eroticism is. *Romance* was made in a state of trance, we were aiming very, very high.

It's an important film, one that is becoming even more important today. I wasn't expecting that it would become even more searing with time.

When my films were rereleased on DVD through Criterion, *The New York Times* did an article that said, "Breillat's films need to be reconsidered in the context of the #MeToo movement." Yes. Except that I didn't conclude the same thing from the #MeToo movement. What I see is a backlash, and the implementation of a ruthless moral order. It's a nightmare. Girls are once again going to be like I was when I was younger: branded as soon as someone makes an inappropriate comment about them. When someone puts their hand on your ass, you have to knee them in the balls, insult the guy. You don't stay there and whine and meditate on your humiliation and then write a book about how you were devastated by it. It's not a big deal, a hand on your ass, it's not a big thing. I'm obviously not talking about violent rape, which you can't defend yourself against, and which is clearly a crime. But we can't confuse rape and the shame one feels from sex where the consent was ambiguous. The temptation to deny it is very strong, you know: you're ashamed of having consented when you didn't want to. So you persuade yourself of having been raped. That mortifying puritanism is dangerous, and I fear that it's becoming the norm.

But when feminists say that shame has to switch sides, that must speak to you, that jibes with your cinema. With rape, the shame returns to the man. Points of contact do exist between you and the feminists.

Of course, except that they say those things but in practice, it's just the opposite. Because when a woman is raped, these days, there's a mandate for her to be raped and devastated for life. I like Natascha Kampusch, she was loathed because she had the nerve to recover after having been held captive for eight years. Society would have liked for her to suffer in a psychiatric hospital, that's what society wanted: they want girls who have been raped to be ruined, traumatized for life. Shame has to switch sides: OK, great! How about if girls who have been raped don't feel shame, and take back their lives as though nothing had happened, while the rapists rot in prison. That, I agree with.

Often in your films, it seems like the men are either boring or else they have a brutal side that thrills you. I don't really see any other kinds of men.

I was raised with Rhett Butler, and I know that you can love men for the same things that you hate in them. It's not worth emasculating them either, they're only men. I love that, that brutishness. My dream was always Rogozhin;[29] I often pursued Rogozhin in my romantic affairs. I would have been better off looking for Prince Myshkin, who was much better in reality, but it took me a long time to understand that. You couldn't be nice to me. I needed antagonism. I needed to fight. All my life I've fought against everything.

It seems like antagonism is the only thing that interests you.

Because that's the way I was built, unfortunately. So there are inevitably things that I'm lacking. My creative process is a tumultuous ferment, that's why I wasn't able to be the great writer that I could have been. I lack reason, the mental construction to be reasonable.

To be able to think outside of oppositions and antagonisms?

That's the way I was built, otherwise I would have become a high school teacher in Niort.

---

29. A character in Dostoyevsky's *The Idiot*, a friend and rival to Prince Myshkin.

You see war everywhere.

I had to. There used to be a quota for advances on receipts. For four advances on receipts, there were slots for three men and one woman. It was awful. But the opposite, parity, is horrible too. I'm a man as Genesis defines man: "God created man … He created *them* male and female." The generic term *man* that human males use to describe themselves is an usurpation. And we're the ones, the women filmmakers, who changed things, not the quotas. Me, Christine Pascal, Jeanne Labrune. Whether they wanted it or not. But to vote for someone because she's a woman, never. I want to be able to be against a woman.

Because you've lived it, that unequal treatment, what prevents you from following your colleagues who fight for there to be, for example, more women in official selection at Cannes?

It's too late for me. It's probably necessary, what they're doing, but I hate anything to do with associations, collectives. And why? Because it very quickly becomes a herd mentality, a singular idea of what is good that excludes everything else. But I'm a lot more flexible than that. I hate when white is white and black is black. It's always good to have more women, more equality, of course, but that can quickly turn, congeal into a block of ice, the terrorism of good versus evil. I carefully blur those lines so I can always escape that. And plus, when you're an artist, you want to be unique, you don't want to be like the others, you want to be one, not fifty.

In Romance, *there's this line: "I really want to meet Jack the Ripper." What does that mean?*

I'm still very fascinated by destruction, self-destruction. Since society mutilates us so much, I want to be able to do even worse things to my body. Their violence is pathetic, and I'm capable of much worse. If I can do worse, that means that no one can ever hurt me. That's the lure of masochism, it may be an expression of absolute pride. If I can do worse, then what do I ever have to fear?

There's also this line in Romance: *"Motherhood is a liberation. They say that a woman isn't a woman before she becomes a mother, it's true."*

No! Not at all. It's ironic, you shouldn't take it in the ordinary sense, but in the symbolic sense. However, as you've pointed out, I have trouble saying I'm a woman. I don't feel it as an identity. Right now, I'd like to say that I'm a man.

I adore my children, but I was made to make films, period. I wrote a long article for *ELLE*, "Why don't young couples want to have children anymore?" I explained that love lives on love and fresh water, and when you have to start to worry about the babysitter, bottles in the refrigerator, diapers, before going out … it's over! I think children destroy couples. Someone gave my daughter the article and she took it very badly. She thought I didn't want her. But I had struggled to get pregnant, I wanted my daughter, I wanted all three of my children. But the fact remains that I am first and foremost, thought. Why must women stop being intransigent minds once they become mothers? I was an amazing mother, but cinema remains my thinking mind, detached from all material contingency. So I'm not a mother, that doesn't define me. Being a mother is a material, not a moral, fact.

The end of Romance *is like a hallucinatory fairy tale that you experience as a sense of relief: Marie is liberated from sexuality.*

Everything is symbolic: the horse, the catafalque, the very small explosion of the building, which had to represent the bigger explosion that we would have had with a bigger budget. But I thought that the husband dying with a little "Pschitt!" was even stronger. And then she leaves with that horse ... You see, when I was little, I had a sort of waking dream: it was the image of a burial with an old symbolic tree, in the middle of a barren moor. I always told myself I'd put that in a film. It was very Bergmanesque. Bergman is my guru, along with Lautréamont.

What would the similarities be between your films and Lautréamont?

Absolute violence, dark romanticism, the despair of destruction, the romantic absolute. Since the world isn't sufficiently pure, it's better to destroy it all. The blaze, and then this vocabulary that's everything I love. The more torture there is, the more I like it. I'm super violent in my imagination but not at all in my life, it's purely oneiric. Words and images never hurt anyone.

The maternal bond eliminates the father, that is felt quite strongly: she found a way to transcend sex in maternity.

Yes, she eliminates the father, it's a sort of revenge. I'm OK with that. I wanted to film the birth very frontally. I wanted to see how I was born. I couldn't ever see before. It was always filmed discreetly from the side. I'm obsessed with being able to see myself head-on. The cameraman almost passed out, because men always pass out at the slightest drop of blood. At the slightest organic thing, they panic. I saw this head emerge like a globe and I understood why the Courbet painting is called *The Origin of the World*: because the baby's head is perfectly round, the veins of the skull are all puffy and blue. I couldn't get over it. It's the origin of the world exactly, it's the earth, our magnificent little blue planet, that comes out of a mother's womb.

Romance is an incredibly cerebral film, feminine and cerebral, and that's what makes it such an important film. When you see it, you're relieved to find yourself whole again, as if you'd been "glued back together." Even so, don't you think the film could still be a turn-on?

The success of the film depends on Marie being an abstraction. That film isn't made to turn men on, just the opposite. If you're looking for that, it's an icy, frigid punishment. José Bénazéraf, who's a jerk, was enlisted to write a review of the film in *Marianne*: me, critiqued by a chic porn director, although he's a total zero, no better than the others! He complained that the actress didn't have large breasts, and wasn't a turn-on, but that's what makes her sublime. It's purity. I like fleshy actresses very much, I adore Marilyn Monroe, but it turns out that *Romance* had to be a blueprint, a theorem. Some men have asked me for a *Romance* for them. Some couples divorced after seeing the film because after that, naturally, the woman changed her opinion of herself. The film acted as a mirror. None of the journalists ever talked to me about my film, they talked about themselves.

That never happened with my other films. Actually, it did, I think: with *Last Summer*.

Is Romance *your favorite film?*

As soon as I finished editing it, I was appalled. I couldn't accept it, accept that I had made that film. I couldn't imagine myself being that glacial and intransigent. I like softness, I like pleasure, sexy women, Marilyn Monroe, Brigitte Bardot. And I could see that there wasn't, deep down, any voluptuousness, only intransigence. I was appalled, it wasn't my film. All that whiteness … It looked like an actual refrigerator. We stopped editing, and it took a month before I could start again and accept the film. And I realized, like in psychoanalysis, that not only was it my film, but it was myself, completely. I had to accept myself as I was. That it be me to that extent was not acceptable. That it be me to that extent meant that it was others, consequently.

The film was actually first called "Frigid Romance."

We couldn't get funding with "Frigid Romance," that was too much of a turn-off even though it was fantastic. I called it *Romance* and I crossed out the word, which created the X of the logo that certain people wanted to put after, "Romance X." But no, that X, that crossing out, which at first was inside the word "Romance," is an ideogram. The X is definitely at the heart of *Romance*, embedded, just as a woman's sex is embedded in her body. Later, I realized that the X is also the female chromosome, and also the unknown quantity (which is feminine) in mathematics.

What did you put in it that made it psychoanalysis?

The off-screen voice, of course. Caroline always did those voice-overs when she was still under the influence of the emotions that came from the scenes. The things she said were almost too didactic, and it could have been horrible. She could have sounded like a pretentious little know-it-all. But with that emotion in her voice, it was serious and touching.

Are you fascinated by your actors when they're right in front of you, or only through the camera lens?

Only when I film them, when I see them—so when I film them. Otherwise, I'm not interested. Samuel Kircher is super charming, I adore him, but what fascinates me are those close-ups, when I enter into him, when I devour him in close-ups. It fascinates me to see his white teeth, his smile. I did close-ups where he let himself be overcome, completely offered up to the camera. I'd never seen that before, never.

So you don't see anything unless you film it?

No, I don't see them if I don't film them. I've always had a horribly scrutinizing gaze. I devour them with my eyes and I've made many enemies with people who can't stand that gaze. I always find material from what's lurking around me. I've always done that: people walking by, I always wonder if they're not material for my films. Understand, films are after all an art form that's made with people's bodies. With painting, there are colors you can buy; with literature, words; and with cinema, bodies. I can't ever say, "The film will be like this." I have to meet the actor, he has to let himself go, get caught, and be filmed. Actors aren't the color red.

CARNAGE

Fat Girl • the little fat girl from Taormina • the
news story of the summer • we had to look outside
McDonald's • young girls playing Rohmer • someone
who isn't seen and who, as a result, sees • it has to
be very AB Productions! • I love Roxane, period •
a point of view is a sequence shot • I rape myself •
I want to be Francis Bacon. I love revolt and surges
of hatred • the commonplace is my favorite cinematic
space • I discovered the absolute pleasure of editing
• fairy tales for ARTE • lots of couples have fewer
things in common than the two of us • the Beast *is*
Prince Charming • I don't beg • *Sex Is Comedy* • I
would have followed any Jack the Ripper

Catherine Breillat: After *Romance*, I especially didn't want to make *Romance 2*, or *Romance 4* … which is what everyone was expecting me to do. I decided to make a small film that would be like a first film.

Murielle Joudet: *Why did you change the original title,* Fat Girl?[30]

Because we organized a *preview* with the people from l'Ifop, something like that, and everyone was against the English title. I imagined the two sisters drinking champagne and toasting their lost virginity, shouting "To my sister!" But no one understood the title, and my sister took it very badly. She actually thought it was a film about her. I should have kept "Fat Girl," which is, for me, the authentic title.

What is the concept of the film?

I was at the Taormina festival to present *Dirty like an Angel*, and when I was there, I saw a young Italian girl with a beautiful face who was doing laps in the pool. When she got out of the water, I saw that she was obese. Her sister was very svelte and pretty, while the overweight girl had a somber, watchful expression—like Bresson's Mouchette. Later she started voluptuously slathering herself with suntan lotion while singing "Tous les garçons et les filles" (All the boys and girls), which I couldn't afford to buy for the film—so I used "I'm Bored," the song that I had written when I was her age. She must have been twelve or thirteen. I asked for her name

---

30. *To my sister!* is the direct English translation of the film's original French title. *Fat Girl* became the film's official English-language title when it was distributed abroad.

and telephone number, which I lost, but I never forgot the image of her. Then, five or ten years later, there was this news story that everyone in the press was talking about: a mother and her two daughters were driving back from their vacation and, at a highway rest stop, they were attacked by a man with an axe. The man came out of the woods and shattered the windshield with an axe. You couldn't make it up. I was at Margaret Ménégoz's house[31] with Toscan, and we were reading things about it constantly, it was the news story of the summer: the man with the axe had more or less decapitated the sister, killed the mother, and you could read between the lines that the younger girl, who was twelve, owed her salvation to the fact that she had consented to giving him a "little treat." The wording alone horrified me. The press made sure, in veiled but evocative terms, that the reader reveled in the details. She had had to undergo an examination at the hospital for them to certify, of course, the damage done to her virginity. The newspapers, the hospital … All of it was awful, like a series of rapes.

Is it not about you and your sister, too?

Of course, sisters are sisters, and I can't not talk about my own. It's a mix between Marie-Hélène and myself, the little Italian girl from Taormina, and the news story. But essentially, I'm both sisters at once.

How did you discover your lead actress, Anaïs Reboux?

---

31. A French producer, the director of Films du Losange.

I told my crew that we had to look outside schools, boulangeries, and especially McDonald's. We came across Anaïs, with whom I felt some kind of connection: there's something that makes a face speak to me, as if it belonged to me, were a part of my family. She acted badly, but I felt this sense of affiliation very strongly. One day, I auditioned all the young girls together, and it was obvious, and ultimately rather embarrassing, that we were looking for a little fat girl. During casting, Anaïs suddenly got into the competitive spirit of it: She's very arrogant, she always has to be first. By herself, she fails, but when there's competition, she succeeds. At the time, I did all my auditions with dialogue from Rohmer films. I listened over the headset to two girls talking together very naturally and I suddenly realized that it was Anaïs and another girl rehearsing. What I thought was conversation was Rohmer's text. That's when I understood that Anaïs was indeed my Anaïs.

The film brought back memories of myself as a young girl, kissing the pool handrail and telling myself love stories. The profound ennui and emotional misery of a young girl in summer.

Really? I didn't experience that, but I was the younger one. The syndrome of the older sister who was a darling before the younger was born, that was familiar to me.

You're the first person to have made a film on that subject, about the emotional misery that a young girl can experience—a young girl who is often filmed as sexual prey, an initiatory body, despite the fact that she may have no experiences and suffer as a result. She's someone who isn't seen, and Fat Girl *is the first time that you've filmed that.*

Yes, I think that it's important to film that, someone who isn't seen and who, as a result, sees. She isn't seen, but she is more powerful in the position of the seer. What the other loses, her sister, is a result of being seen. And all the critics kept saying that the character of Roxane's was an idiot: as if being beautiful, as if letting yourself be innocently manipulated by a seducer means that you're an idiot. But we've all been like that!

Why were you interested in putting this obese body at the center of a film?

I was very withdrawn when I was little, very arrogant. I wanted to film that, a young girl locked up in her body.

The film begins pretty cruelly: no one is watching her except you, and she eats her banana split while watching her sister kiss a boy, as if she were watching a film—which could be 36 fillette—that she will never experience.

Anaïs was very intelligent, she knew what she was acting. It wasn't violent for her, and anyway, she wasn't self-conscious, not in the least. Instead, she had a superiority complex. And then again, she's big, but she's beautiful. And she got along marvelously with Roxane Mesquida.

That was your first collaboration with Roxane Mesquida.

I spotted Roxane right away. I had to use a girl who was at least sixteen years old, otherwise the films couldn't enter the foreign market. So she absolutely had to be sixteen during the shoot, but I didn't want her to be Hamiltonian, with pigtails, either.

So I only saw girls who were fourteen or fifteen, who looked much older on camera. And suddenly, Roxane showed up, and the casting director thought she was too AB Productions,[32] but I love that. There are plenty of scenes where I said, "Now, here, it has to be very AB Productions!"

She's the actress you've worked with the most.

When I met her, she was definitely eighteen, but around fifteen, mentally. She was abnormally immature, as dull as dishwater—but brave and super reliable. She's become this delightful, cultured young woman. I love Roxane, period. I recently had dinner with her, she told me that in Los Angeles where she lives, certain newspapers were calling her up to ask if she had anything nauseating to say about my film shoots. They insisted on getting their scoop. But that's the zeitgeist.

Many of your films are structured around one long sequence shot. When, for you, is a sequence shot called for?

Cinema is a point of view, and a point of view is a sequence shot. Whenever there's fear, or emotion, you need one. You enter into the shot, you follow a path and arrive at an emotion that's in the midst of unfolding. If you have to cut, and pick it back up again, it's a catastrophe. That's how I did the sequence shot in *Fat Girl*. I thought, "How can I get my actors to undress?" I violate myself to achieve what I've written in the script. And then it's so hard to get actors to undress that you

---

32. AB Productions was a production company and distributor that focused on children's cartoons and music.

don't want to tell them twice. That's when I say to myself: "We'll do it all in a single take; that way, they won't bother me with refusing to undress!" My nightmare has always been that the actors haven't understood that they have to be naked in a certain scene. When they tell me that the makeup artist did their whole body, not only their face, it's a total relief, because it means that they've understood what they have to do.

Do you think about the sequence shot while you're writing the screenplay?

No, I only think about it when I'm faced with a problem. I can only envision a sequence shot with a specific problem in a specific location. I'm always looking for how actors can move around in a particular space; I move through it myself and end up figuring it out.

A Real Young Girl, Perfect Love, Fat Girl, Anatomy of Hell … *You often end your films with carnage.*

I love that. After all, I'm a woman who started making cinema in an era when they talked about "women's films": delicateness, modesty, and feminine refinement. And I wanted … *scratch!* A man's thing. All the men I adored and read were about absolute violence and misogyny, like Lautréamont. You couldn't ask for someone more misogynistic and violent. Henry Miller, Rabelais: I love the opposite of the image people want to assign me. I don't want to be Marie Laurencin, I want to be Francis Bacon. I like revolt and surges of hatred. From an artistic point of view, that's gorgeous. The artistic act isn't mannered, it's violent, whether you like it or not.

In general, how did advances on receipts for your films go?

It required tenacity. Usually I would have to postpone; I never got it on the first try. They would table me and I'd rework the screenplay. I always had people who adamantly supported me, but the people who hated me were typically more numerous. I presented *36 fillette* six times, I exhausted three presidents. This time Christian Bourgois, my ex-editor, told me that the long bedroom scene wasn't cinema, that I had to "leave it out." And so I, quite rightly, think we can't cut it out, we can't leave out what seems commonplace: the commonplace is my favorite cinematic space. It's precisely the site of denial. We think we know but we don't, and we especially don't want to go and look and say what's really happening.

I was rereading the very severe remarks that Yann Dedet made about you. He says that the scene in the hotel room is too long, that you didn't want to cut it and that you made the scene "as televisual as possible."

Well, there you go! In *36 fillette*, he cut a sublime scene too short. That's just like Yann Dedet, and that's why he's only Yann Dedet. I don't know why he's bad-mouthing me, but I'll bad-mouth him—even though we got along very well. As an editor, Dedet uses all his knowledge and his genius to artificially reconstruct another film, because he knows how to make connections: instead of a certain character coming first, he'll make him come last. He twists the film, he manipulates the story, he's very skilled but it's all nonsense. He was a very, very good editor, but his genius consists in working miracles of technical ingenuity, to say to himself, "I, Yann Dedet, am making another film with the material I've been entrusted with." It's a very bad approach.

What's the right approach?

The editor who scrutinizes, who listens to the film and finds himself in every frame. Who asks, "Where is the film in all this?" Searching for the film, realizing the film that was shot, not the one that wasn't shot, which is what Yann Dedet did. On *Last Summer*, I was so anxious that I didn't let François Quiqueré edit by himself; I was always there. It's a pleasure, a joy to edit with someone who's an absolute virtuoso, who remembers the slightest smile that's missing, that we weren't able to edit. I always asked him, "And what about this, can't we put it in?" He made *jump cuts* that I didn't even notice. He's brilliant, he has a certain simplicity and an unbelievable ear. He's glued to the image, he knows everything, he has the film in his head. He's a great editor.

Do you enjoy editing?

During *Last Summer*, I discovered the absolute pleasure of being there in the editing room from morning until night. I missed out on that pleasure before that film—Francois revealed it to me. He showed me that there's a kind of incredible pleasure in working together, searching, saying, "'Let's go back a little; there, look, there, there's a dimple, there's a light in the eyes, that's what I want!' 'Right there, I like that.' 'I don't want that! I told you I didn't want that!'" There are images I love and images I can't stand. Before, I had unknowingly deprived myself of editing my own film without sacrificing any of the images I liked. When you sacrifice an image, a glance, it means the rhythm of the film is off.

Do people talk about your films made for television?

My films for television? But they made the rounds of all the festivals! And they were released in theaters in the United States. I consider them to be full-fledged films.

Ah, yes, sorry. Incidentally, I discovered your cinema with Brief Crossing *(Brève traversée), which aired very late at night on ARTE during my summer vacation. Today, television isn't in a position to finance that kind of story, right?*

Not for me, at any rate. The new people never want to do what the older ones did. I actually was supposed to direct a trilogy of fairy tales. After *Bluebeard* (*Barbe bleue*) and *The Sleeping Beauty* (*La belle endormie*), I was hoping to direct *Beauty and the Beast*. ARTE had said yes, then Jérôme Clément left,[32] along with the guy who was in charge of TV movies. Véronique Cayla, who liked me a lot, became the boss. She wanted me to do something like *La minute vieille*.[33] No thanks, I don't beg.

Beauty and the Beast *is very you. How did you want to film it?*

---

33. Chairman of the board of ARTE from 1989 to 1999 and from 2006 to 2011; succeeded by Véronique Cayla, who served from 2011 to 2020.
34. Created in 2012, this series is done in a short, two-minute format that features elderly women telling what are often dirty jokes and making other comments that are in stark contrast to the image they project.

It is *the* subject for me. No one has ever talked about or filmed what's really interesting in that fairy tale, that's why it's *my* subject. What needs to be said is that in reality, the Beast is the prince: we see him as a beast, but he is Prince Charming. The Beast *is* the dark object of desire in some way. It's the sexual attraction that you don't want to admit, so it takes the form of a beast to which the Beauty is very attracted. I'm the only one who can say that, the others are kitsch, except for Cocteau, who is obviously sublime.

Sex Is Comedy *was initially a project for television.*

Pierre Chevalier asked me to make a film for the ARTE series Masculin/Féminin,[35] so I wrote *Sex Is Comedy* over the summer. Jean-François Lepetit was very enthusiastic about the screenplay and wanted to make it with me as a separate film in itself, not for television. He told me, "I'll give you a lover's quarrel, even though we're not lovers!" I answered that in a certain way, yes, films are a little like our children. There are lots of couples who have fewer things in common than the two of us, so I finally decided to make *Sex Is Comedy* with him. I had the screenplay for *Brief Crossing* in my computer, it was a commission for a miniseries on the theme of the brief encounter—but Didier Decoin was fired and the series was canceled.[36] So I brought it to Pierre Chevalier, who was very pleased with that screenplay … Jean-François always called *Brief Crossing* an "illegitimate

35. A French radio, cinema, and television producer who spent twelve years as the head of fiction at La Sept ARTE, a golden age during which many filmmakers directed some of their most beautiful films and thrived within the constraints of a small budget and the TV format.
36. A writer and screenwriter who spent three and a half years (1992–95) as the president of fiction at France 2.

child," he was sick about it, and he was right. Actually, I think I prefer *Brief Crossing* to *Sex Is Comedy*.

In Fat Girl, *the reverse shot is from the point of view of the fat girl, watching Roxane Mesquida. In* Sex Is Comedy, *you're the one who's observing Roxane. Why did you have to make a film about your work and your method? Was there a need to theorize and explain your relationship to actors?*

I always wanted to tell a story about a shoot, because it's so very dense and passionate and people don't understand what it is. The real title should have been "The Making of a Sex Scene." How do you shoot a sex scene? People have all these ideas about stars, nude scenes, glamour … Except that it isn't nudity I'm filming, it's intimacy. I film ultraintimacy. I want to be *there*, between the two actors, to have the impression of sleeping with each of them—but also with the camera. What really bothers the viewer is when you film that, the ultraintimate, it has nothing to do with the fact that the actors are undressed. Staying so long on the faces, that's what troubles people, that's what so displeased Yann Dedet. And on the set it's troubling too, everyone is very troubled because it's very intense.

In Sex Is Comedy, *Jeanne (Anne Parillaud), your alter ego, says while discussing a sex scene, "I don't have the right to be there." You could say that that's the mantra of your cinema as a whole, the mantra of all your great scenes: you don't have the right to be there, you impose yourself.*

The first time I understood that was during the scene in *Dirty like an Angel* where Lio has her panties between her ankles.

Brasseur is masturbating her; even if you don't see it, you understand it very clearly. And on Lio's face you can see the confusion, shame, and anger that she feels at being so carried away by her own desire. It was so incredible to film that: catching that naked face tears out the soul, it doesn't just mimic a love scene. I had the same feeling in *Fat Girl*, with the big seduction scene that lasted twenty minutes.

You like that feeling of being over the top.

Yes, it's terribly beautiful, magical. But I don't want to spy through the keyhole, that's voyeurism, that's salacious. I want to be there, in the room. I'm obsessed by that, filming what someone's like when they make love.

Your cinema is constructed on this tilt between the clothed world and the unclothed world.

Yes, that fascinates me. When there used to be absolute sexual freedom, after the pill and abortion, before AIDS. In that era, you could go with any guy you wanted, and it could end badly, you could be murdered. I always kept myself from doing that, I was afraid, but I think that I would have followed any Jack the Ripper. That could be fascinating.

RED BLOOD IS WHAT'S REALLY BEAUTIFUL

Anatomy of Hell • Rocco, *c'est moi* • I've never left a knife on the table • what's most beautiful about ourselves • one man giving another man a blow job, it's much better that way • ready for the psych ward • a turtleneck actress • like Shylock • if I need a goat, I'll use a goat • carpet cinema • no one makes a film for the audience, they do it for the audience's money • The Last Mistress • it has to be said over and over again, horror is absolute beauty • black diamonds do exist • between *Barry Lyndon* and *Thérèse* • everything has to be sublime in a movie dress • I hate extras • he realized that they were two different worlds • a film is very prosaic, very pathetic

Murielle Joudet: *The text has never been so visible, palpable as it is in* Anatomy of Hell—*it's as if image and text act as equals.*

Catherine Breillat: At first, I wanted to adapt Duras's The *Malady of Death* (1982). But Yann Andréa wanted to keep the rights for Josée Dayan, with Jeanne Moreau in the role of Duras, and wouldn't sell them to me until after the film was completed. For me, the idea of going after Dayan was the ultimate insult. I thought, "Well, after all, I know how to write, so I'll write my own *Malady of Death*." I was thinking more about Lautréamont than Duras: the curses, the metaphors.

You've always said, "Rocco, c'est moi."

Yes, there's a resemblance, as Anaïs says to her sister while looking in the mirror: other, but of the same family. I had that resemblance with Rocco, with Fu'ad,[37] with Anaïs Reboux, a little with Samuel Kircher. It's essential to my films, and I don't necessarily see myself in a girl. With Rocco, the impression of doubling was so strong that it was sometimes annoying—I was filming myself. His green eyes like mine. And like me, he's the one who watches, he has that male violence that I've always loved and that makes me who I am. I'm fascinated by rape, that's obvious, I wrote a song that I never recorded, "Rape Field." The words were, "And take me to that hazy field, where the sky plays with the waves. And take me to that rape field." Like a fatality.

What fascinates you so much about rape?

---

37. Fu'ad Aït Aattou, an actor in *The Last Mistress*.

Horror mixed with vertigo. The tipping point: everything's fine, you're in control of yourself, and then all of a sudden, you've turned into a news item. I find that absolutely fascinating. Like the idea that you could gouge your eyes out at any moment. Then, life becomes a disaster. It can become that at any moment, it's that simple, so sudden. The tipping point, the vertigo of the tipping point. That's why, at home, I've never left a knife on the table, I'm too scared.

Have you always felt that things could tilt at any moment?

Yes, I could be in my bedroom in Bréhat and then I'll go down and put the knives away in the drawer. People are always very surprised because I have lots of butcher knives at home, in all forms. And also ancient daggers, slightly barbaric, inlaid with semiprecious stones. I brought one back from Lithuania, one from Israel. The scimitar in *Bluebeard* was mine.

Did you want to make Anatomy of Hell *to rectify the coital shot that you didn't put in* Romance?

I wanted to remake *Romance*, but this time *in the mud*. I'd only done it in the ether, because I was always afraid of tarnishing Caroline. With *Anatomy of Hell*, I hired a porn actress for the explicit scenes. So the body was split in two once again, but I cleverly glued it back together with kinetic splices, not inserts. The book that I adapted was called *Pornocracy* (*Pornocratie*),[38] no one understood that title: *pórnê*, in Greek, is "a woman" or

38. Catherine Breillat, *Pornocracy*, trans. Paul Buck and Catherine Petit (Semiotext(e), 2008).

"a courtesan." In ancient times, the Greeks regretted the importance that women had in democracy. They bitterly resented that courtesans could manipulate men and determine law from their bedrooms. Pornocracy doesn't mean the reign of pornography at all, but the reign, the political reign, of women.

You say that as a filmmaker, you are tied to a "pornographic imperative." What is that?

Since every filmmaker just gives up, since they delegate what's most beautiful about ourselves—namely, sexuality—to pornographic cinema, I have to take care of it. The imperative is to say: "No, that's not the way you make love." It's showing that the filmmaker's gaze transcends all of that, that it isn't about pornography, that something else entirely is going on.

Where did the idea to put a woman in front of a homosexual come from?

He isn't a homosexual, exactly. He defines himself negatively: I showed him as "a man who doesn't like women," he wants to kill them. And for me, that encompasses all men. Since I'm probably a bit sadistic, it amused me to stick Rocco in this setting of a gay nightclub. I wanted him to prove his love for me, for my films! When the film came out, he only worried about one thing: What will the press say when they see him playing a homosexual? That club, it's humanity, it's men who love and admire only each other. Liberty, Equality, Fraternity.

The movie opens with a blow job.

That's the fraudulent side of men. It's the men who enjoy it, as far as I'm concerned! And people pretend that women can take pleasure in it. Not for me! If you do take pleasure in it, that comes from conditioning: you get it into your head that it could give you pleasure to pleasure a man. But in terms of actual pleasure, there is none. It's a mental pleasure that's been put in your head. But one man giving another man a blow job, it's much better that way. It's coherent.

It reminds one of Romance *quite a bit. The actress is like a brush you use to draw a series of tableaux, images. Her hallucinated image every night.*

I meticulously designed the sets, I did all the costumes. Notably the vision of the coral necklace formed by dripping blood: he thinks he wants to save her but deep down he wants to murder her—the image articulates his compulsion. The violence of men against women is, after all, extraordinary.

You also evoke King Kong *(Merian C. Cooper and Ernest B. Schoedsack, 1933).*

Yes, when he passes his hand through his hair with all that sticky gel, that's King Kong's hand. I adore that film, with King Kong completely fascinated by the little woman in his hand— it's totally and absolutely *Anatomy of Hell.*

Why does the man want to kill the woman?

Because he ends up loving her and it's unnatural, it's unbearable for him. He smears her, he degrades her, he does everything to her, even though he doesn't even know her name. She crucifies herself to tell him what he is, but also to reveal to the man what a woman is. She knows who she is. When all he has left is the sheet, and he comes back wearing it like the shroud of Christ, he understands that he has murdered her.

What were your choices for the film's cinematography?

The night before the shoot, my assistant said to me, "Catherine, check out tomorrow's work schedule," and then my world collapsed. I was on the verge of a nervous breakdown: What had I done, what had I written for myself? It all seemed unfilmable to me. All of it. I was distraught: the menstrual blood, the lipstick on the anus … You'd have to be insane to do that. How to do it? How to do it so that it isn't horrible? I was ravaged by anxiety, I hid behind my sunglasses, I was ready for the psych ward. Then when I get to the set, like always, I feel great, my inhibitions disappear completely. My fear of myself disappears. I know nothing about light, but I said to my cinematographer, Yorgos Arvanitis: "I think that we have to treat it as a black-and-white film, except that it's in color. You have to think 'silent film,' except it's full of talking. We're going to make a silent expressionist film."

You had already met Amira Casar during the casting of Romance?

Yes, and right away I told her that she was perfect for me, but unfortunately she wasn't right for *Romance*: I needed an actress who seemed virginal. But the seed was sown: we knew that we were made for each other. For *Anatomy*, I had finally decided on a very pretty young actress who looked a bit like she came out of a sitcom, a Sarah something who ultimately told me that she didn't want to do any nonsimulated sex scenes after all; she was afraid of ending up at the psychiatrist's office. That was obviously not my intention, but I want to make my films in my own way, and that's my absolute right. Amira also refused the idea of sleeping with Rocco. I told her that I need my actors to give me something, I need my pound of flesh, like Shylock in *The Merchant of Venice*.[39] They can't come out of the shoot totally unscathed, otherwise the film would turn out totally sanitized. Rocco gave me the gift of playing a homosexual. But she didn't want to. So OK, if I have to use an actress who doesn't want to do the sex, I'd rather use Amira. My producer didn't understand how she ended up on the film. Desire. It's called desire. You have to like the actors and they have to like making the film, that's how it works, it isn't rational. You have to tell yourself that the people who quit a film were quite simply not the right ones. The film always finds its interpreter, it's a kind of miracle.

Was it difficult for her?

Making the film wasn't hard, but making it with Rocco was. To her, he wasn't an actor—she was the actress, she was the one who had to act well, while he was the Beast. The first thing she said when she saw him was "Rocco, I'm using a body double." He was devastated: "She thinks I'm the Elephant Man." He thought that if they didn't have sex, the whole thing would be phony. He only understands what he calls "true." I told him,

---

39. William Shakespeare's *The Merchant of Venice* (1600): To help out his friend Bassanio, a merchant named Antonio borrows money from the usurer Shylock. Certain he will be able to pay him back, Antonio signs a contract in which he authorizes his creditor to take a pound of flesh from him in the case that he defaults on his payment.

"Rocco, you're going to learn that you can't pretend to feel feelings and emotions, they're going to have to be real. In cinema, acts can be false, but not emotions." He came to understand that beyond all of my expectations, and Amira was quite surprised to see that he was so good. That reassured her.

She defined herself as a "turtleneck" actress, and for *Anatomy of Hell*, she had to be naked with her legs spread practically all the time. She was afraid, and that's only natural. It's the worst film you could make with me. Amira made it out of love for my cinema, but it was terrifying for her, as it was for me. I was ready to abandon certain scenes that in the end turned out to be the most beautiful ones. It's always like that: the most dangerous, the most unspeakable, they're often the most beautiful. For me, the worst scene is the one with the Tampax full of blood, but that one, she was actually very happy to play!

I can understand how that might not be the most terrifying scene.

Well, for me, that was an absolute taboo, having a period, a body, a sex. Hiding under huge dresses to conceal your pregnancy, not showing that you look like a fat cow. Hiding all of that crude and organic stuff that men don't want to see so they don't get disgusted—and even without that, just thinking about it makes them disgusted in advance. That's how I was raised. I got my period when I was twelve, and I had large breasts in a society that forbids us from having them, because they're thought of as teats. I remember that when the first issue of *Lui* came out, it was a mutilation: to see Sophia Loren in a horrible, slutty slip, it was terrible. Why do stars need to be photographed like that for men to jerk off to? I was really humiliated by that. And all of my cinema comes from that, from the fact that I don't want that erotic image. The exciting lingerie, the garter belts, let them jerk off all by themselves with that! That's not how I want to be desired. I was raised in a bath of mud, or shit.

That's what you see in the film, when you talk about that flaccid, flabby flesh that disgusts men, even when we get rid of our body hair …

Yes, that skin that doesn't even have the decency to be green! Like those ads for maxi pads where they pour blue water into them. But you know what's really interesting? Not lavender-blue dishwater. Red blood is what's really beautiful.

Even if a woman shaves, it's still going to show, she'll always be marked by her hairiness. What side are you on? Are you disgusted by hair, too?

Oh yes, I'm antihair—for men, too!

Those are the two parts of your brain that dialogue between each other in the film.

Yes, because what you've been taught stays with you. I'm against it, but it remains. I exorcise it, but it remains.

You ultimately made the film with a body double for the explicit scenes. You were willing to have a body double for Amira Casar and not for Caroline Ducey?

Romance's project was to flout the prohibition of filming nonsimulated acts. If Caroline had refused, I might have found the solution in a body double. I also might have gone back to using Laure

Marsac. It's perhaps utopian to make a film with nonsimulated acts, because above and beyond that challenge, not only do you have to create cinema, but beautiful cinema. I found Godard's rejection letter after I had offered him the role of Robert in *Romance*, dated March 3, 1988. He had handwritten, "Dear Catherine Breillat, after thinking about it, I realized that I had already answered this question thirty years ago." And below that, he had taped a newspaper clipping dated November 1966: "I will never make the film I really want to make, because it would be impossible. It would have been a film on love, or about love, or with love. Speaking inside the mouth, touching a breast; for women, imagining and seeing the man's body, his sex, caressing a shoulder—things that are as difficult to show and to understand as terror, and war, and illness. I don't understand why and it pains me."

I think it's both astonishing and terrible that the pope of French cinema died without having had the courage to make the film he dreamed of making. It's devastating to see how he kowtowed. With the same thoughts in mind, Ōshima decided to make *In the Realm of the Senses*, and he said, "To make this kind of a film, you have to stand on the border of the abyss." Godard invokes war, horror, and illness to justify his renunciation of sexual representation! It's terrible. He was mired in a terrible vision. I made *Romance* specifically to go against that deathly vision.

Caroline Ducey may have blamed you for attacking pornography while casting a porn star as the lead actor.

Rocco was the only one who could have done it: a "normal" actor wouldn't have been able to get hard, and plus, Rocco is smarter than everyone else. It's always about morality and moralism, but I make cinema. If I need a goat, I'll use a goat. If I need a man I hate,

I'll use a man I hate. I would even be able to make another film with Asia Argento if I ever needed her for one of my films. Actors are material. You have to see things for what they are. Yes, it's totally immoral to realize one's fantasies with actors' bodies. I recognize that, but it's sacred because art is sacred. So it transcends morality.

For you, is a shoot a matter of seizing control, or is it a loss of control?

Both. I wouldn't be able to stand making a mediocre film, so I have to fight so that it doesn't become grotesque. And I write scenes that are on the threshold of the impossible; they're impossible to shoot. On a shoot, I never say to myself, "I'm going to do this, then this, then this." The first thing I ask is, "How could I have possibly written that? How am I going to get out of this?" The carnage at the end of *Fat Girl*: how do you film a man who comes out of the woods and shatters a windshield … How, *how* do you film that? Generally, the answer comes in the middle of the night, in a trance, otherwise I can't do it. "How do I handle this?" That's my question. With *Last Summer*, it was: "How do I handle shooting a love story with a fifty-year-old woman and a boy who looks barely seventeen?"

Making films is getting yourself out of trouble.

Yes, yes.

In your book of interviews with Claire Vassé, you talk about "carpet cinema."[40]

Oh yes! Bourgeois cinema, even if it's not necessarily bad. What was his name again, that big carpet cinema director?

Claude Sautet?

Yes! It's cinema that takes no risks. You win without risk, you triumph with no glory. That's what carpet cinema looks like. It can be good, sure, but is that really what's underneath relationships, underneath the underneath of relationships? There's no harshness there. Life is much more harsh than that.

You film a bourgeois couple in Last Summer. *How do you film bourgeois worlds without becoming bourgeois?*

I don't do sociology, not at all. I film bourgeois environments because I require a relationship to language, and educated people. In *Last Summer*, Saïd Ben Saïd told me that I had a Pasolinian side, but it's only my imagination that's Pasolinian, I don't film boors like he does. I need absolute civilization and I need its relationship to language. I film Perdican[41] or the young Werther, not Accattone.

You've said, "Back then, the imperative was to do what the bourgeoisie couldn't stand, and the actors agreed to do it." Today, would you say that actors have crossed over to the bourgeois side, that they don't want to do anything anymore?

Of course. Hiram Keller, who acted in *A Real Young Girl*, was a star, and when I asked him to do unimaginable things, he never asked questions, he just did them. Back then, they believed in

---

40. Catherine Breillat, *Corps amoureux: Entretiens avec Claire Vassé* [Loving bodies: Interviews with Claire Vassé] (Denoël, 2006).
41. The hero of Alfred de Musset's play *Camille and Perdican* (*On ne badine pas avec l'amour*) (1834).

cinema; today they believe in the box office, and the last thing they want to do is shock the audience. But they never really make a film for the audience, no one makes a film for the audience, they do it for the audience's money. Don't confuse the two. I make films for myself and I agree to tear myself apart, provided that in the end, I'm not ashamed of myself.

Still, you say that a role can have psychological consequences.

I said it in *Sex Is Comedy*: that's why actors are paid so much more handsomely than us, even though they work so little! They make four films a year, and we barely make one. We work night and day and are paid a pittance compared to them. And since they are paid more than us, they have more power than we do. You think they don't hesitate to pick up the phone and complain to the producer or their agent that people aren't being nice to them?

Should actors work more?

No, I would never ask that of them. It's ugly work, that's clear. I'm asking for grace, which is work on oneself. Making a film is like entering into Carmel, that's what it's like. It's a sacred and sacrificial ceremony: of course actors sacrifice their souls, but it's a sacred sacrifice that they have to move through. Today it's only about money and contracts, so they forget the substance of their profession, which is to be an actor. They primarily want to be stars. Every art is absolute suffering and joy, all of the arts. You think that pianists, great musicians, and everyone who makes art on an extreme level, you think they don't suffer? Only suffering can bring the ultimate joy of having succeeded.

After Anatomy of Hell, *you did a series of three literary adaptations:* The Last Mistress, Bluebeard, The Sleeping Beauty. *Did anything change when you were developing a film from someone else's text?*

No, nothing, because I'm carnivorous, so I appropriate everything. Everything becomes me. I always thought that I was Barbey d'Aurevilly, a dandy who broke all the taboos of the era, all the prohibitions set by the Church; he even risked prison for it. He kept himself right at the limit, without ever crossing it, like me. *The Last Mistress* is my dream, it's like all those stars from the '50s, those femmes fatales, that's what I wanted to film. And plus, Ryno de Marigny is me: that's when I started to become my male characters. When the Viscount de Prony sees Ryno's carriage with Ryno's coat of arms ostensibly left at Vellini's door and says, "If he ever becomes minister, unpopularity will be his glory," that's obviously me.

It was your first film after your stroke. How did you finance it?

Like always, I make films with much less money than other people. *The Last Mistress*, a period piece, had the same budget as *Little White Lies* (Guillaume Canet, 2010)! I wanted to make the film ten years earlier, and I had the advance, but I let it go to make *Romance*.

Did you ever think, after your stroke, that you wouldn't be able to make films anymore?

No, just the opposite. Just before the stroke, I had wanted to make *Bad Love* and I was in preproduction for *Bluebeard*; I was going to shoot it two weeks later. In the hospital, Jean-François

Lepetit held me in his arms and persuaded me that we were going to make the film. I said to myself, "This guy is crazy." They were making me arrange cubes into a rectangle and testing me to find out if I could tell the difference between a man and a woman. They didn't know if I was going to be able to walk again, let alone shoot! I was haunted by the idea that I could only do the most essential things, so I wondered which film to make. Was *Bad Love, Bluebeard*, or *The Last Mistress* absolutely essential? That was the question that tortured me, because I didn't have much more time to live.

Did the hemiplegia change your mise-en-scène?

No. It was exhausting, though. Before, I waged exhausting little turf wars and I couldn't do that anymore. So I started to become more solitary during filming. On the shoot of *The Last Mistress*, I had a little bed: every time between shots, when they had to adjust the lighting, I went to sleep on my little cot, even if only for ten minutes. On the shoot of *Last Summer*, I asked for my bed but I didn't need it, it was unbelievable. At night I slept on set, in the couple's house, I haunted the scenery and spent my nights inventing the way I was going to do the next day's scenes and how I was going to manage to get myself out of it. I would never have been able to find all the magical solutions I did find if I hadn't slept on set. When the crew arrived in the morning, they were always quite shocked.

What's so beautiful about The Last Mistress *is the rigor mortis that the actors have: Fu'ad Aït Aattou is deathly pale, bloodless. They're pallid vampires, as if their blood is no longer circulating. I was thinking that you often do that, you film beautiful cadavers.*

I love transparency. Fu'ad has an incredible complexion, with his enormous green eyes and that Béatrice Dalle mouth. I love the complexions in paintings from the sixteenth and seventeenth centuries. When I was ten, or twelve, I was stupefied by the altarpiece of the Maître de Moulins with that livid Virgin, her almost bluish skin.[42] When I was sixteen, I would squeeze lemons over my skin to make it even more pale, I would draw veins, I loved absolute pallor. I'm always on the lookout for transparency: the skin that Amira, Roxane, Samuel, Fu'ad had. At the end of *Last Summer*, Samuel's body is so white that it's like a seventeenth-century painting. The final love scene is totally asexual, it's completely and utterly divine.

Given your taste for absolute transparency, I wonder if you could film actors who weren't white.

Of course, I was supposed to shoot with Naomi Campbell. I would have loved to, there's something pure about her. I would have found something; after all, I'm not a fetishist. She wrote me a little note—in the United States, they like me—and I realized that she wanted to shoot a film with me. I set a trap with my assistant. I had decided to do the auditions at the last minute, to know for sure. I told her, "If you don't know how to act, if there's nothing happening on camera, it's not even worth it." All while reassuring her that I wasn't going to keep the screen test, since Campbell's image is very valuable. She arrived, looking impeccable, and was due at the UN immediately after: we did an improvised scene and she was sublime in it, in tears, all her makeup streaming down her face. That's the only thing I'm looking for, that purity,

---

42. The triptych of the Maître de Moulins (1502), attributed to the painter Jean Hey, can be found in the Cathédrale Notre-Dame-de-l'Annonciation in Moulins.

people who believe in something else, something greater. It's not the whiteness of someone's skin that interests me. I simply ask that people be like crystal, and black diamonds do exist.

In The Last Mistress, *there are scenes in which you love filming the immaculate whiteness of someone's skin and, suddenly, blood flows, surging from a gash. Blood stains the whiteness: the film seems to function according to this principle.*

I love that, I love beauty that's been murdered or violated. It's in the book. I adore blood and violence. It has to be said again and again that horror is absolute beauty.

There's a whole passage where Ryno de Marigny and Vellini live out their passion in Morocco, and it's stunning, very pictorial, even though it was shot on a budget.

Painters always save me. I had a ton of Orientalist stuff, silver belts with antique stones and caracos embroidered with gold that I'd bought thirty years ago in Turkey, absolutely sublime costumes. I love fabrics, I can't help myself from buying everything I see that I think is beautiful, and these fabrics were on the ground in the street in Ephesus. I thought that I was going to dress Asia in a very Orientalist way, very in vogue at the time. In Brittany, we had used up our four-day exemption from the Île-de-France—they were participating in the financing. So we could only travel locally. In the book, I think they go to Switzerland and Lake Como. I suddenly thought of Orientalism: they would travel to Algeria. I only needed to find a big sand dune, just one, and that would be the desert. We picked out a large dune in the Sablières de la Seine, and at the top we built a small hut. I reproduced it almost exactly from a super-famous watercolor painting by Delacroix. I just added a goat.

One shot, one tableau. How do you avoid being consumed by the period film? How do you keep it from becoming the production designer's film?

It could never; production designers, they design. And I set a rule: everyone walks around naked under their clothes. Wearing costumes is natural. Next, only use beautiful things. I wanted to make a film somewhere between *Barry Lyndon* (Stanley Kubrick, 1975) and Cavalier's *Thérèse* (1986). Kubrick also shot in ruined castles, he didn't rebuild them, he made do. I did the same because who cares? What matters is imagination, poetry, not the accuracy of the reconstruction. People are much too Cartesian when the poetry is right there, under our eyes. Life isn't like that, everything of a piece, there's always yin and yang. The horrible is always intertwined with the sacred. Everything is intertwined, darkness with light.

And in this case, you weave reconstruction with ruin.

I know a lot about French art. I know things, I can talk about them, so everything was open to me, I even obtained the right to shoot in the Salon des Singes, in the Archives Nationales, where there's the most beautiful woodwork in the world. Normally, that's not allowed. I'd go from room to room and visualize the sets, which I brought together in one place, I transformed it into Cinecittà. I maintain that I had the most beautiful costumes in the world in *The Last Mistress*. All the lace is from the nineteenth century, in spider silk, made by hand. Even at the time, that cost an absolute fortune. The softness of that silk against a face, that's something quite different than machine-made silk. The tortoiseshell fan, the jewelry ... it's all real. The seal is a real gold seal from the eighteenth century, the gold embroideries are all authentic. Only real things. I decided to donate all my costumes to the Cinémathèque: Bluebeard's cape that's worth at least €500 or €600, the cup from which they drank chicken's blood, €200 or €300 ... I know my stuff, and I buy everything.

Where did you get this knowledge about costumes?

I've always loved fabrics passionately, and I only need to touch them to know that they're beautiful. At the bottom of an enormous bin full of fabrics, I only have to pass my hand through it to find the beautiful one. And when the fabric is beautiful, the color is beautiful.

What's your favorite fabric?

Linen. Once I had an Armani jacket in waxed linen, it never wrinkled, never. When people say linen wrinkles, it isn't true. Only poor-quality linen wrinkles. In *Romance*, I wanted wool etamine, which costs an absolute fortune. We managed to find a coupon from CHANEL, and an ex-master couturier from Dior cut the dress that I designed myself. I wanted fat folds like you see in paintings, something extremely pure. Everything was made by hand.

In fact, you're not filming actors, you're filming fabrics!

Caroline Ducey understood that right away. She knew she had the part when I had her try on a red dress that I had bought many years before, thinking that it was a movie dress and that one day, I'd end up needing it for a film. The dress was perfect on her. Red means something, it cannot be mediocre. Everything has to be sublime in a movie dress, especially a red one.

What do you consider to be the most beautiful film costumes?

In Rimini, I saw Fellini's costumes. They were rags, but the illusion was created cinematically because he was a genius: all of a sudden, it becomes a vertiginous fashion show. He's really the king of costumes. Visconti was also never wrong, he was a prince after all, and princes know what's beautiful, beautiful woodwork, beautiful châteaus … They're never wrong. They're not going to tell you that Versailles has parquet floors! They know how to tell the difference. And then, I also love *Gilda* (Charles Vidor, 1946), the '50s, Dietrich, Hayworth, Marilyn, of course. Those actresses, that's my dream. Marilyn is so dazzling that you'll watch a film just for her, which means that it's *her* film. She eclipses the director. She is the film!

You've said that the budgets of all your films put together could fit into the budget of The Last Mistress. *Would you like to have more money? What would you do if someone gave you $20 million for a film?*

I'd make two. Or, like Godard, I'd pocket half and direct two films with the rest, even three! But ultimately I need urgency, fear, and dread at the idea that I'll never be able to do it, that I can't do it, that I don't have either the time or the money and what's more, I have to do even better than everyone else with less. And plus, I'm too lazy. I told Saïd Ben Saïd to give me one month to write the screenplay for *Last Summer*, not three.

Things only start to happen at the last minute. People don't understand, they think we're shooting scripts. But there are things that other people do that I don't know how to do, like managing a thousand people in one scene—I have no sense of space. So I do things in small spaces, I'm a director of close-ups. I'm autistic, so I'll go on talking endlessly to someone, whereas at a cocktail party, I never know where to put myself.

You never film a busy street, everything is always very empty, with very few extras.

Extras are very expensive and plus, I basically hate them. Because I don't know how to direct them, I hate them. And it's much more beautiful without them. Still, I knew how to manage the extras in *The Last Mistress* in the sequence at the church: I decided that there would be a big cross, and I absorbed the extras through the belly of the church. For the opera scene, I counted them one by one and decided that you'd never see the performance, so I framed twenty-six extras down to the millimeter. I never use an over-the-shoulder shot: I look at things so much that I don't want to film an actor looking at something. No, his gaze is the camera's! If he's the one watching, then he shouldn't be in the shot. An over-the-shoulder shot is realism, whereas I'm in the realm of contemplation. The actor must be the camera, watching.

Why bring all your actresses together?

In his dreadful TV show, Laurent Ruquier had the gall to say to me that all of my actresses hated me, and I wanted to show that that wasn't true, that they all wanted to work with me again. A ballet master is very hard on his dancers, it's very hard to reach the pinnacle. But how exhilarating it is to reach it! You're thrilled—thrilled. I was very tough during *The Last Mistress*, but not with Asia, who understood the nature of the role so well that I didn't have to do anything.

Do actors interest you outside of shoots? Do you ever see them again?

No, because they're not speaking my words, so they're no longer mine. I only love them when they're mine. I want them to speak my sentences, perform my gestures, and then I love them. There isn't time to see actors again. I only love Rocco when he's mine, when he belongs to me, when he does everything I want.

Are you still in contact with him?

No … I remember when we stopped filming for a week on *Anatomy* so that he could attend the porn industry's Oscar ceremony, in Las Vegas, where he scooped up all the awards. When he came back, this extraordinary, stunning actor had had enough time to become a lousy porn actor again. In the night-club scene, he wasn't good at all. I was devastated. He noticed, he realized that they were two different worlds and that he couldn't simply move from one to the other. The next day, we had to shoot the critical scene where he starts crying in the bar. He spent the entire night walking through the streets of Lisbon. In one night, he shed his porn-actor skin to become my actor again. Simply by spending a sleepless night walking the streets.

You also find solutions in the middle of the night.

It's the moment of despair. Basically, a film is very prosaic, very pathetic. A series of small realistic actions, libidinous and stupid. And then, throwing a camera in front of people to film them, a priori, has no chance of working. But when it does work, suddenly, it's dazzling.

DANCING WITH THE BULL

Abuse of Weakness • I wanted to kill myself every day • I may walk like RoboCop, but my films won't be disabled • a mangy dog • a traumatizing language for the body • you're taught to love the man who kills you • the perfect flop, the ideal son-in-law • Huppert is a masterful woman • my job is to be a tyrant • two monsters on that shoot • my goal is to get to the faena • Verhoeven and Cronenberg • it was like the first steps on the moon • I, me, it's cinema • how I am is also how others are • *The Cloven Viscount* • I love cinema too much to do catharsis • the landscape doesn't have to recognize itself

Catherine Breillat: I started to feel very comfortable with my disability once I decided to be like Stephen Hawking: a larval brain with transparent eyes. That solved the problem. I don't worry about how people see me anymore, they can hear me, and that's enough. In the beginning, I had a recurring dream that resembled this scene in *The Fearless Vampire Killers* (Roman Polanski, 1967): I dreamt of a coffin that was hurtling down a mountain at top speed, and BOOM! the coffin went directly into the garbage. That was a recurring dream that I would pursue when I was awake. Obviously, the body was me. Don't think it was self-destructive, or cruel. Simply lucid. Good riddance! It was a very good thing, it gave me back my soul.

Murielle Joudet: *What does that dream mean?*

That I don't have a body anymore, and that I have to get used to it. As a child, I really identified with Riquet, the hunchbacked prince from Perrault's fairy tale. No princess would marry him, then one day a princess looked at him with love and proved that deep down, he had always been Prince Charming, only no one had ever really seen him. The gaze constructs you: if people look at you wrongly, they disfigure you. The way disability is seen is atrocious.

How were you able to construct the narrative of Abuse *of* Weakness *when the facts, for you, still seem unreal?* [43]

I have clarity about every moment of my life, and I know every detail: the words, what I hear, what it was like. I remember

---

43. Catherine Breillat, *Abus de faiblesse* (Fayard, 2009).

everything and I make use of it continuously in my films. But with this, even now that I've recovered, I still don't know exactly what happened. I was under the influence of the rape drug, I was taking Rivotril in high doses to prevent severe epileptic crises: they were potentially fatal, caused by my bleed scar. Actually, that's why Christophe Rocancourt was convicted. And that's also why, perhaps, I have no clear idea of what actually happened. I didn't know I was even taking that drug until the trial happened. The book had to be mainstream to warrant the advance that allowed me to survive that whole saga. The father of my younger son helped me out financially, my sister, too, but I had nothing.

Is that why you cowrote the book?

I wanted it to have readers, so I had to get out of my esoteric writing style and for that, I told Olivier Nora, the CEO of Fayard, that I needed a ghostwriter. He proposed that I do the book with Jean-François Kervéan, who's an intellectual and a very good writer. I went to his place every day, and we were a good match; we had lots of things in common and his apartment was totally my style. I told him my story, often in tears, often asking him if Christophe Rocancourt was sincere at the time or if he was lying to me. I was totally lost. I understood nothing about what had happened to me. I adored his first chapter; it was written in a style that was so much simpler than mine. So much simpler. But from the second chapter on, it was unbearable. I couldn't cosign that, I'd rather starve! We decided to go together to my house in Bréhat and started using a different method. I wrote first, with my vocabulary, my vengeful aphorisms, and my unbearable digressions. And at night, he put all of it in order. We worked nonstop, it was exhausting and exhilarating. After a month, the book was written. Olivier Nora thought it was incredible, "almost too good for it to be mass-market," he said. The book had moderate sales, but at least I'd gotten a check and had temporarily survived. For two, three years I wanted to kill myself every day, but I told myself, "Today is another day." I tell myself the same thing when it's going badly on a film.

You write about your hemiplegia, "I had become this body that was other people's labor."

Yes, I couldn't do anything, couldn't dress myself, or drink, nothing, I couldn't eat, nothing. I lived at Rocancourt's place for four months, my arm was broken, I was totally isolated from my family, I was taking this Rivotril. I was, as Sonia Rolland can attest, a sort of zombie. I woke up to eat my breakfast and my overdose of medicines, then I went back to bed. I woke up for the next meal, and went back to bed. Sonia was an angel with me. Curiously, even though she's a thousand times younger than me, I thought of her as my big sister, my mother, and my guardian angel.

You say this magnificent thing: your mother cut you in two horizontally, and the stroke did the same thing vertically. Is that how you perceive it? Do you see the irony of an ordeal that could only happen to you?

It happens to me because I can bear it. All kinds of disasters happen to me, but I can bear them. I'm stronger than them. It's pretentious, but it's true. After my stroke, I had decided that I would never complain and maybe I was wrong, I should have complained a little. I wasn't completely strong enough to manage alone. It's not only the Rivotril that explains the Rocancourt saga, but a psychic fragility that takes root once you depend completely on other people. Being a hemiplegic, that forces you to be close to another body in a way that, typically, never happens in normal life, and I had a lot of trouble with that. I have to hold on to another person's arm, I need help putting my boot back on, I get tangled up in my clothes ... When I made *Abuse of Weakness*, I simply wanted to make a film that wasn't disabled. I wrote a letter to a critic who had the nerve to write that I was very diminished by a stroke, I told him, "I may walk like RoboCop, but my films won't be disabled." That's the most important thing. I'd rather be disabled than have my films be disabled.

You say in the book that with Rocancourt, you had glimpsed the possibility of a great story. You threw yourself into the jaws of the wolf out of the desire for a story?

But I've "thrown" myself into the jaws of every possible wolf! I'm not healthy. I'm always very good at giving romantic advice but when it comes to myself, I make every possible mistake. Rocancourt is garbage and even if I am the victim, I don't want to be victimized. And plus, he wasn't a wolf, he was a dog, and I wasn't able to see that he was also a mangy dog. At the time, I wasn't very familiar with the laws. I didn't know that the law had changed, and that bad checks were no longer a crime but a debt.

You get the feeling in the film that this guy, played by Kool Shen, is a sort of remedy to boredom.

Back then, I couldn't go outside, because if anyone even brushed past me, I could fall. He came every afternoon and took me out, took away my boredom ... And then, I had made *Police*, I had seen gangsters, real ones, guys who would burn the bottoms of your feet with a blowtorch to make you talk. What I didn't know is that the real thugs still have a code of honor. I wasn't suspicious of Rocancourt, he didn't scare me, he was white bread to me. He had everything to lose by falling back into scamming: his daughter; his wife, Sonia, who was sublime; his apartment. Everything.

What was more traumatizing, the stroke or Rocancourt?

Rocancourt, because I don't know what happened to me. The stroke was an enormous physical trauma but, mentally, I know what happened to me.

Why did you choose Kool Shen to play him?

I didn't want him to have Rocancourt's gigolo, dandyish side. But I have to say that he's got something ... He has to have something, because he isn't intelligent at all, just wily and perverse. I have to admit that he had a trace of adolescence in his boundless narcissism that was pretty charming. And a very sexual sort of thing, a way of occupying space. I thought a rapper would know how to occupy space. The problem with French actors is that they don't know how to walk: I saw DiCaprio walk across the room to go onstage, and it was a real trajectory. He inhabited the space. Ask a French actor to do that, and after you slate the shot and it's like the slate is following him behind his back. Nothing about him is natural. I have a theory about that, actually: If the French are totally inhibited, it's probably because of our language. French is classical music, while every other language is modern music. When French people speak patois, they're comfortable in their own skin. When someone speaks French—that language that's so subtle and rectilinear—their movements are inhibited. After Libero De Rienzo[44] had learned French perfectly, his acting suddenly started getting worse. He was much more pinched; it's very interesting. It's a traumatizing language for the body and its freedom of movement—totally stilted. You can't talk about money, you can't talk about anything.

We can talk about sex a little, can't we?

Yes, but always in a lewd way, not in the way it should be talked about. So I started watching rappers on the internet, knowing nothing about them. I thought JoeyStarr was amazing, but he wasn't right for the role. I met Kool Shen, I decided to *vouvoyer* him [use the formal means of address], saying to myself, "Well, anyway, he's a rapper." It was between him and Samuel Benchetrit. Kool Shen had more body, but there weren't four lines in a row that rang true. It felt like caricature to me, because he hated Rocancourt and made him despicable. I called him back and did something incredible, something no one would normally put up with: I showed him his audition scenes and Benchetrit's, saying, "He's better here, you're better there." Then, "You despise Rocancourt, but I can't despise my character." I gave him the long scene from *Fat Girl* to learn, which is super literary, with very long sentences and plus, it's a very

44. An actor in *Fat Girl*.

bourgeois situation, very Marivaux. He had a lot of trouble with it, because he wasn't used to learning lines. He was sitting in a club chair, and when my assistant fed him the lines, then he was magical. You didn't feel the text as lines, he simply spoke. I had him redo the scene so I could be sure, and the same thing happened. He was my actor, and he knew it right away. On set, he was brilliant, very intelligent, he understood everything. He played from his gut, without any intellectualization.

I have the impression that your actresses play from their brain, whereas with your actors, it comes from the belly, between the brain and the belly. The acting has to come from two different places.

I've never thought about it that way but maybe that's true. But it's unconscious, because I don't fundamentally understand men. I only understand them if I put myself in their skin, if I say "I." I'm very autistic when it comes to men.

You have an appetite for big brutes.

Yes, that's my whole problem. Bluebeard: you're taught to love the man who kills you, and you tell yourself that unlike everyone else, you'll be OK. I told myself the same thing with Rocancourt. Rogozhin, Rhett Butler: you're taught to love the domineering chauvinist who definitely loves you, but mistreats you.

You don't think it would be good to fall in love with nice boys?

If you gave girls nice boys to fall in love with, they wouldn't pick them, and they don't exist anyway, so the girls would be depressed about not finding anyone. The perfect flop, the ideal son-in-law, they're a pain in the ass, women don't want them! It doesn't matter if men are the way they are, it's women who aren't equipped to deal with macho chauvinists. It's the image of women that's poorly constructed. I remember this MP talking about another MP who had put his hand on her ass: she was miserable, she wrote a book about it, everything was a nightmare, she was in tears … And Christine Angot, who had actually been raped by her father, yelled at her and told her to be strong. Well, yeah! We need strong women to counter the chauvinists. To get a hard-on, men have to tell themselves a story about how strong they are, how much they dominate us, but it's a story, a fantasy. They need that and we can't blame them.

You had wanted to work with Isabelle Huppert for a long time.

She had turned down *Perfect Love* and I wanted her to act in *Sex Is Comedy*. I went to see her at the theater. After the performance, the corridor was packed with people and I made eye contact with Anne Parillaud. I said to my assistant, "She wants to make a film with me."

Huppert didn't want to do the film?

She hesitated and she wasn't wrong to, it's very complicated to play a director who only thinks about her film and the image of the actress when you're an actress yourself. I only understood how complicated it is to film the work of a filmmaker after I had started shooting. Actors are caught up in films: they don't make them, they don't see them. On the set, I never knew if I was shooting the heroine's film or my own, there were no reference points to speak of. And since I didn't have any money, the crew who acted in the film was my own crew. There was no boundary.

How did you convince her to do Abuse of Weakness?

I called her and I said, "Isabelle, if you want to work with me before I die, it's now or never, either you do the film or you'll never work with me!" She accepted.

Did she need to do a lot of preparation to perform all the choreography of broken gestures? Opening a packet of ham, walking, eating ...

No! Because that's the way I open my pack of ham. I only had to show her what to do to manage with only one hand, almost like a dog.

Did you torment her a little on the shoot?

My shoots are always very difficult at the beginning. You have to strip away everything that's yours to become what I want. Then, once everything is in place, it's pure pleasure and I say practically nothing, I'm just in awe of my actors. I don't want to be the tyrannical master, I want them to enthrall me. I want to get gaga over them. Huppert is a masterful woman: she can dive deep into a role but then, the second the scene is over, she becomes herself again. Other people would have been damaged by the role, but not her.

Many witnesses have told me that you yell at the actors, notably at Isabelle Huppert, who remained unfazed. So I'm starting to think that it's probably true.

It's true, during takes, I talk! I talk all the time, I don't even know what I'm saying, even if I can say things that are very, very harsh. I often say that my job is to be a tyrant, and when there are two tyrants on set, you have to deal with the problem. The only tyrant that should be there is me: I am the director and even Huppert has to do what I say. There's no other way. So definitely, at the beginning, it was a clash of the titans. When she saw the film, she was super happy and I asked her, "But Isabelle, wasn't it a little too hard for you?" She answered that yes, every day she asked how she was going to finish the film. I was stunned: "But after all, Pialat, when he said such vicious things to you, that you had as much talent as Annie Girardot, that you were an aging actress, that was worse!" She said, "No, you're much worse!" I was really happy.

You wanted to be the worst, in fact.

Yes, but it was so delicious, and after all, it only lasted the first two days. We were two monsters on that shoot, it was either her, or me. When she tried to impose her rules, I told her in an icy voice that I could stay at the hotel and she could direct herself—I'd be happy to pocket the money. If I'm there, if I make the effort to get up even though it's a pain in the ass, then I'm the one in charge. She was shocked that I'd redo takes because she's used to only doing two, so I told her, "With me you'll do fourteen!" Fourteen, that's the ritual number I give actors, that means that we have all the time in the world, it doesn't matter how much film we use up.

What do you say to actors during scenes?

When I was editing *Last Summer*, I heard myself on the rushes: in reality, I direct actors, I throw intonations at them. Same with Isabelle: I gave her lines with the tone I wanted—I realized that. Huppert said to me, "You're giving me line readings! That's out of the question!" I shot back, "Come on, Isabelle, I'm not giving you a line reading, I'm getting you in frame." But in fact, I do give line readings, I can't help myself, but I need to stop. I shouldn't think that I'm always right. There are times when my actors are much better than I think. I berate them even though they're amazing. I look at the rushes and I think, "What an idiot! Can't I shut up?" But that's how I work, I can't do it any other way. I'm so anguished by the idea of not reaching the peak because I'm too soft, that sometimes I'm wrong.

There's a bit of sadism in all of that.

Maybe, I recognize that that may be true. I don't know, I don't know. I know that I take possession of my actors. At the beginning it's the whip, and after that it's all love and they're radiant. But for them to be radiant, it's imperative that it be hard at the beginning. I compare it to bullfighting: my goal is to get to the faena,[45] that moment when the toreador dances with the bull. I have to demolish the praise and their certainty that everything they do is good. You have to make the bull bow his head, otherwise there won't be any faena. The spears are the least beautiful thing about bullfighting, it's carnage. And why does the toreador spear the bull? To make the bull bow his head, otherwise there's no bullfight.

---

45. The third act of the bullfight, the faena.

Yes, but in the end, the bull is the one who dies.

When the toreador engages with the bull, he can also die.

One of the two has to die.

My crew loves me. If I were so extremely unfair and cruel, they would never forgive me. You have to understand that. I can be very mean, but it's always with a specific goal, which is the film. In the end, Isabelle was doing fourteen takes, I couldn't stop her, she was having so much fun.

She surrendered to the film?

Completely. At the beginning she had demands, like being able to watch the playback, but I don't like actors to watch themselves: if they think it's good, they just try to copy it. I'm the eye, I'm the one who transforms, it's my gaze that I want, not theirs. But since she's a star, the young girl who was working the playback gave in to her demands, so I scolded her, saying that no one is allowed to see it. Isabelle answered that she had never worked on a film where she didn't see the playback. "Well, this one you won't see, it's not in your contract!" That belongs to me, that's my domain. But it was a major crisis.

What's your favorite film with Huppert?

I don't know if I really love French filmmakers, but I do love *Loulou.* I like her in Chabrol's films: he knows how to film her, he really loves her. *The Piano Teacher* (Michael Haneke, 2001) is too symbolic, I much prefer Verhoeven, he's more my type.

Elle *(Paul Verhoeven, 2016) and* Abuse of Weakness *have a lot in common.*

When *Elle* came out, I had a screenplay on my computer that was called "Lui." I was inspired by a news story: the story of a very brutal rapist who, right after the attack, became tender again. He started having a very romantic relationship with his victim, and then suddenly, he turns around and rapes her again … and then treats her as a lover.

It's totally Verhoeven's film.

Yes! My cinema is very close to his. Actually it's funny, because Saïd Ben Saïd produces the people I'm closest to. I'm very much in line with Verhoeven's cinema: the brutality, the humor, his hatred for eroticism, exactly like me. The taste for, the fascination with destruction, *Basic Instinct* …

There are lots of rape scenes in Verhoeven.

Yes, and I adore that! It's assassinated beauty, it's a work of art. I love garbage dumps, slaughtered landscapes. I could see that *Elle* was the same screenplay as "Lui," that we were twins in some way. Cronenberg too, *Crash* (1996), *eXistenZ*, those slimy objects that inspire such disgust in us, it's done so that we ask ourselves why we're disgusted—that was at the center of *A Real Young Girl*. It's sexual repulsion, obviously. I've done several panels on censorship with Cronenberg, he actually defended me against censorship in Ontario. We have something similar in our deceptive, rebellious, clinical relationship to sexuality.

Abuse of Weakness opens with your stroke and ten minutes that summarize your grueling rehabilitation, but everything is very beautiful and stylized: a body learning to walk again.

It's a dreadful shock when you realize that you can't put your foot down on the ground without falling. During my rehabilitation, I was determined and I didn't want to be treated like an invalid. I remember that the nurse acted as if I were a really famous person who wanted to be treated differently than everyone else, so they had to put me back in line and treat me even worse. They wanted me to eat in the canteen, to stay with everyone who was in the same state as me, for us to stay parked there all together. The only thing that connected me to the world was the sky I could see out my window; if they closed the curtains, I would start crying. And then there was the telephone, and music. The nurse would come in to turn it off—to her, Horowitz was noise. I have an immense respect and gratitude for nurses, but there are also *Kapos* who take advantage of the fact that you're disabled, and at their mercy.

What did you learn during that rehabilitation?

I expected that the rehabilitation would be about physical gymnastics, but in fact, it's mental, it's purely a matter of concentration. On that front, I was way more gifted than other people. An intellectual can be retrained more quickly, people who aren't brainy don't make it, because it involves engaging neurons that have gone dark, and programming them to make movements. You can make spectacular progress and then, suddenly, regress. It's very discouraging. A young child is retrained very quickly, and almost totally, because her brain is still made for learning, creating synapses—a function that weakens with age. I remember the immense gratitude that I felt for the nurse who made me take my first step. It was like the first steps of the man on the moon, I was terrified of falling. I had to believe absolutely in what he was telling me, to believe, in a religious sense, that I could hold myself up on my left leg, that it existed, even if my brain didn't know where it was. We were riveted to each other's gaze, our two hands outstretched. You have to have absolute confidence, and throw yourself into it. If I had fallen, besides the fracture, the loss of confidence would have been irremediable. Then I had to learn endurance, like a baby. Learning to walk again means learning to have absolute confidence in another person.

It's true that the film feels like a kind of space exploration: very white, clinical, visually lunar. During your rehabilitation, did you think that you'd make a film about it?

No. I'm not one of those girls who wants to make a film about her cancer. I rehabilitated myself, they took care of me, and Jean-François brought me films to watch. I asked him for *Crash*, which I watched on a loop, I loved it. When I broke my arm and I had a steel bar screwed into my skin, I was really happy, it was like in the film. I thought I should be wearing Yamamoto. There's something very cinematic in the torture of the body.

The scene where you design your orthopedic boots yourself, saying, "It doesn't have to be ugly!" sums up the film perfectly. How did you avoid getting sucked into making a hospital film?

I'm the one who designed the boots, and they still make that model! It's not the hospital that matters, it's me, it's the body. I'm the one who's in my body, I'm the one who inhabits spaces and transforms them. The real is what's microscopic. What's beautiful is what's true. I only film intimacy, with others or with myself. I'm the only one living, I live with myself and I don't want to be someone else. I could tell myself that other people are lucky, that they're young, not decrepit like me, but no—I'm me. I'm not interested in being other people. Not at all. Quite simply because they aren't me. When you're madly in love, you think that you won't be able to live without the other person, but in fact you can, you can. You only ever live with yourself, always.

What's the borderline between that understanding of self and narcissism?

I am very egocentric, after all. The difference is one's contentment with oneself: I'm not content with myself. I can be happy with a film, but always anxious: I wonder if the bar is high enough, if there's another filmmaker out there who's better than me, and you know, there is!

Did it do something to you to revisit that period, and to film it?

No. There was only one scene that was pretty terrible, and that was when I showed Isabelle the exercises with the physio ball. Those exercises were terrifying. Every time I couldn't do it, I burst into tears, because it seemed so insignificant and simple. You never get used to not being able to do elementary things that any two-year-old could do. There was also the scene with the stained bathrobe, where Maud is supposed to cry. I told Huppert, "You're in bed, you're crying," and then I started crying and couldn't calm myself down. I'm a big crier, I have crying jags like epilepsy fits—after twenty-four hours, you feel like you're about to die. I talked about Maud in the third person, it was Maud, there's no way it could have been me.

"It's me, but it wasn't me." That's what Maud says at the end to her children.

Well, yes, it would be impossible, if it were me ... it would be unbearable, I'd start crying, I wouldn't be able to do anything. So I said to Huppert: "Now, you get up and start crying again." And then I started crying again. Isabelle was panicked: "Catherine, you're the one who should be playing this scene." No, you're the one, and you're going to do it beautifully. And she did the exact same thing, it was magical.

It's the only film where we see your children, they pick you up at the end of the film like a little girl after she's done something foolish. Mom did something foolish.

Yes, completely. They had nothing but contempt, no compassion at all. Paul's father is the only one who understood.

Clichéd question: Was the film cathartic?

No! Everyone thinks that. Or else I'm hiding something from myself, but I don't think so. For me, it was cinema, period. I, me, it's cinema. That's the only thing in the world that I love. My kids blame me for it, and then you've told me that I never talk about being a mother in my films, that I understand. I absolutely love my children, but if I don't have cinema, who is there to love them, if I don't have an "I"? The "I" is cinema.

You don't believe in catharsis? In purging yourself of your passions?

Not at all, not at all. No! I'm really about "know thyself," I want to see what I am, see and *make others see*. How I am is also how other people are. The more sincere I am, the more I describe in explicit detail, the more I tell other people's stories. We all live the same life, with the same feelings, failures, faults, whether small or large. But that doesn't make us despicable people. I can't stand people who are only good. I love Italo Calvino and *The Cloven Viscount* (1955). It's a very short book, a fable: the story of an awful, mean, cruel viscount who is totally without pity and hated by his subjects. He leaves to go on crusade and gets cut in half. The good half returns: He's nothing but kindness, you couldn't dream of having a better overlord. No flaws, full of empathy, charitable, wonderful … But after a while, his subjects end up not being able to stand him, to the point that they miss the old viscount. Because at least, before, they could hate him.

I think that's what life is like. People who are totally pure terrify me. And cinema is there to explore that right not to be all black or all white. I agree with Calvino: if something's totally black, you can hate it, but if it's totally white, you can't hate it, you can't do anything, it's simply superior to you. That's the effect the Left always has on me, actually: I prefer the Right because at least you know all of its flaws and you can't buy into it. But at least you know what you don't like. You don't have to say, "Oh, if I could only be like that!"

Is Abuse of Weakness *a film about love, for you?*

There was an ambiguity there, I agree. When Rocancourt slept at my house in that little bed, it was hysterical, we talked to each other through this wall … At the time, I could sense the beauty of the dialogue, it was really a scene from an American comedy with Audrey Hepburn and Cary Grant. In the morning, I'd rush to write it all down because there was a kind of cinematic perfection to it. But there was still this ambiguity: watching myself experience something I relish as a cinematic scene, and not understanding what's really going on. But one thing that's certain is that making the film was not a catharsis, I have too much respect for cinema for that. And it upset me that everyone thought I was making a therapeutic film—all the journalists wrote that, but I love cinema too much to do catharsis. With *Abuse of Weakness*, I was taking back control, making cinema again with a wonderful subject. Fiction is simply a change of medium, nothing more. I used to say that to the criminals I'd gone to see for *Police* who thought I was a snitch. I told them that if they recognized themselves in the script, then it was art, like when a great painter sets up his easel in front of a landscape. Once the landscape is on the canvas, that's the art. And if he doesn't like it, the landscape doesn't have to recognize itself.

THE AMOROUS CAMERA

Last Summer • a completely Florentine eyelid • from Caravaggio to Raphael in the same shot • the cut of the century • like a ghost poisoning their imagination • that's obviously Marnie • you needed that something, that overdose of age • young man with pearl teeth • he asks me to chisel his diamond • drool, tears, snot • that shot is my life's dream • you're young and you're going to die of your first love affair • the slightest thing will spoil the imaginary perfection of the shot • a real ad for Cartier • you can never be too explicit with idiots • conjugal love is beautiful, even if it's boring • no one cares about old people • I'd have to do it as a Netflix series • undressing, penetrating, that seemed impossible in everyday life

Catherine Breillat: Saïd Ben Saïd wrote me an email, reminding me that we had met at the Belfort festival three years before; he told me that he had purchased the rights to remake a Danish film, and thought that I could do a better job of it.[46] Me, make a film? Me, who had been retired for almost ten years? I was finished, forgotten, a has-been. A priori, my vocation isn't making remakes, but rising from my own ashes. I saw the film and was blown away by one scene, the moment when the stepmother lies to her husband, and absolutely denies having had a relationship with her stepson. That scene only works by establishing denial, which is the subject of all of my films. In short, it was something to do, and then an assignment, that's always an invigorating challenge. I didn't change very much in the screenplay; I kept some of the dialogue almost word for word, and yet the result is nothing like the original. In my film, the adolescent is the one who wants the affair. I didn't want her to be a predator, but a woman trapped by the love of an adolescent. *Last Summer* is a textbook case: starting with two nearly identical screenplays, the two films have nothing to do with one another.

Murielle Joudet: *I remember that one day you were very worried. While you were editing, you hadn't yet found the story the film was telling. How did you get out of that?*

It came gradually, by sculpting the film in the editing room. First you make a draft, then fill in the details. I had filmed Samuel Kircher with such starry-eyed devotion that I thought I had made a film about adolescence and not about Léa Drucker at all. But in fact, it's filming Samuel so intensely that eroticizes

---

46. *Last Summer* is a remake of *Queen of Hearts* (May el-Toukhy, 2019).

Léa, that renders her so beautiful and moving. By hiding her, I ended up revealing her even more because then, she emerges like a diamond. François and I were very surprised.[47] A film is a very obscure thing. The screenplay is one creation, and the editing its recreation.

I'd read the screenplay of Last Summer, *and I'd seen the Danish film, but your film is something else, something I hadn't anticipated. I wasn't expecting the extent to which the film would be consumed by Samuel Kircher. It's clear that you fell in love by seeing images of him, not him in real life.*

I had an all-devouring passion for him. It's the day we did his close-up that I really saw it. In real life, I'm not in love, but I love him; when he's in close-up, I'm in love. I'm constantly saying this, but I'll say it once again: the gaze is a transfiguration, and that's why I love to do it so much. When someone loves you, they make you beautiful. When they make love at the very end of the film, when Samuel leans his head against the logs, I could see that his face had been transfigured. His lips became defined, swollen with blood, magical. He looked like Lorenzo Lotto's portrait of an adolescent boy that's hanging in Bergamo.[48] It was so beautiful, that limpid, abandoned, transfigured face. A completely Florentine eyelid. I told him, "Tilt your head back, a little higher, toward Léa!" And then, it was totally a painting. Miracle, miracle, miracle. I did the color calibration with Jeanne Lapoirie,[49] I told her, "You know, Jeanne, I've seen several

47. François Quiqueré, the editor of *Last Summer*.
48. Lorenzo Lotto, *Portrait of a Young Man* (ca. 1500), collection of the Accademia Carrara, Bergamo.
49. The cinematographer of *Last Summer*.

different versions. Normally I don't like too much contrast, but when you have a white body against dark logs, the contrast is beautiful. I wanted the body to be a Caravaggio but the face to be a Raphael, that soft light that Raphaels have, with pink skin. Jeanne said, "Oh, fine, I just have to find a way to go from Caravaggio to Raphael in the same shot!"

I was afraid that the film would only be about one thing, but it's about five at once: the buoyancy of youth, a family unit ready do to anything to defend itself against what threatens it, crazy love, bourgeois denial, the last passion of an icy woman ... Meaning is always left open, and continues to open even further.

It's exactly the same as *36 fillette*: this absolute contradiction between our desire and our morality. In the name of desire, we put ourselves in impossible situations. But if desire isn't fundamentally moral, it isn't fundamentally libidinous, either. For me, it's always about scrambling the reference points of right and wrong. Those markers do exist, but never on the level of sex and desire—except for rape, of course, that we know. But when you reach that degree of ambiguity, you don't know anymore. Relationships are murky, made up of too many things that we don't want to admit. In France, the country of Musset and Marivaux, we should know that. I love that in cinema, it's immediately obvious: everything that you don't want to admit becomes blatant once it is projected on the screen, and then everyone understands. In literature, I would have had to add a "but" to describe what, in cinema, you can see on a face. I just love that.

You repatriate everything to the territory of love, and we don't even want to moralize about anything anymore.

I make things in a black fog. I hadn't planned for the ending to be *Camille and Perdican*: Samuel reporting and threatening her. Léa saying, "It doesn't constitute incest because I'm the one who gave in." Then Samuel follows Léa into her office to try to freak her out, but we understand that all of it, all of the threats, was nothing but the language of lovers, a love scene. At first, to her, it seemed like threats, but no, it wasn't that at all: he rebels because she threw him away like a Kleenex, it's amorous pride, he didn't give a shit about the financial agreement. It's a relationship where, all of a sudden, someone gets hurt and desperately wants the other to come back.

There's that magnificent, very mischievous scene: Samuel's face is between Léa's legs and he asks, "Am I making progress?"

It's a sequence shot, but I did the reverse shot in the mirror, and I was extremely proud of that. I absolutely wanted to see Samuel say, "Am I making progress?" but the idea of cutting the shot to do a reverse shot horrified me. I thought about it all night and in the morning, I said to Jeanne, "Look, if I've put a mirror at the head of the bed, it's probably for good reason, it's not an insignificant thing!" That was my solution: do the shot/countershot in the mirror. It was such a complicated shot that Jeanne nearly fainted, but in the end it worked. It was actually very difficult to transition to that sequence shot from the previous scene, when Samuel and Léa are on the grass with the Dictaphone. Moving from the close-up of Léa in tears to the close-up of Samuel's head between her legs was an impossible cut; with François, we called that "the cut of the century"! I have to be careful with myself, though, because I write very easily but I don't shoot easily. It's simple, I don't know how to shoot the mundane. Everyone's better than I am when it comes to filming everyday life.

Still, you have the tartines at breakfast ...

I love eating scenes. I love how people ingest things into the body, wolf them down without any sort of embarrassment. I don't understand how it can be an ordinary thing, when it's essentially animalistic and totally indecent.

How did you get the idea to put Samuel in the background of that scene, lurking behind the window?

I thought of it at the last minute. The scene bored me, because it's one of those quotidian sketches that aren't my strength. I shot it first without him, it was fine but I was bored. And since I'm never bored filming Samuel, I asked him if he could skulk around behind the window, not knowing what to do with himself. That scene only takes on depth and ambiguity once Samuel is behind the window, like a ghost, poisoning their imagination. Cinema is always a mystery. If I had written that, people would have laughed in my face: you only understand what you need to do once you're doing it. You have to do what you're not supposed to do, and you have to do it when you want to. That's what counts, the wanting. The only thing that's really interesting is doing what can't be done. It might also have something to do with Samuel's languid body, like a white, mute eel, a prisoner behind aquarium glass.

It seems as if you empty your films of everything that's real. How do you drive it out?

The real overwhelms and blinds us. Reality is everywhere, we know it by heart, and it only leads us into things that are conventional and already understood. Truth is the important thing. Something that's much more invisible but overpowering that takes up all the space. We're molded by symbols from birth, in double meanings and details, and that's what makes everything important in a film. I do everything, I'm an obsessive and an absolute maniac. The colors, everything. On *Last Summer*, I did it all, I made all the decisions, down to the slightest detail. With Khadija Zeggaï, my costume designer, she's a genius and I adore her, we chose just the right fabrics, and made very special dresses with a '50s cut. We also went to the flea market to find a style of shoe that I'm obsessed with: '60s stilettos with a round heel. They're harder and harder to find, but I think I'd like to have them for all of my films; the fact that the heel is round, it goes with the whole body.

That's not something that corresponds with a particular character?

No, I don't care about character. It's as if you said that in such and such a painting, some detail goes with a particular character. Saying that makes no sense. The moment it becomes graphic, it already "corresponds" with the character and with my style, especially. Do you know what experts do to authenticate a painter's work? Well, it should be the same thing in cinema, you should be able to authenticate a filmmaker's cinematographic *écriture* just by seeing a few images.

It's my understanding that you decide on everything, even the sets.

Sets are costumes too, the colors have to be exact. Mirrors everywhere, because it drives the cinematographer crazy.

Mirrors are always helpful. The absolute worst thing in cinema is when actors, as soon as they start talking, go in profile. You always have to keep actors from going into profile, while minimizing the use of reverse shots. Except when they're face to face, and it's antagonistic. Then you can, because the viewer must always see what the other sees.

You never film in profile?

No! It's natural to be in profile, but then I don't see both eyes. To get the emotion, you have to have the face in front of you, you have to *see* the face of *that* body. And the face of that body is the gaze, it's the close-up. I use them systematically, and call it "the lover's camera." It's an incredible emotion, being able to achieve that closeness that you never get in life. In life, you don't understand each other, but suddenly, with cinema, I can achieve intimacy, a kind of absolute comprehension that is also beauty. Nothing is ever ugly.

How have you directed your actors?

I hate the expected: if someone plays my scenes just as it seems I've written them, then that bores me, I find it conventional. I want something else, something different from what other people ask for. I told Léa and Olivier Rabourdin, "I'm hearing the comma, that's not what I want." I completely choreograph them, the slightest glance: even a blink won't be acceptable to me, or a frown, or even worse, the raising of eyebrows—I don't want that. Or talking too fast because you want the scene to be over with. Actors always read too fast, but cinema is slowness. I'm always asking my actors to slow down their gestures, to speak slowly, to move less quickly. I need to scrutinize, I need poetry, so it should be slow enough to see things, and for everything to tip over into expressionism.

They shouldn't blink?

Never! And I furiously tell them, "You're not concentrating, that's why you're blinking!" You can't act, forget about actors who act. You have to *be*, deliver real emotions, the ones you feel in life. Being an actor isn't about acting, it's feeling. So yes, I am tough, I'm not saying ... When I say to them, "Cry!" there's no way it won't be in a second. Understanding what I want is always very disturbing, because I break everything, all the acting that's acting. I only want truth and poetry. And in the end, they radiate bliss.

There are lots of different screenplays in Last Summer: *the Hitchcock screenplay, Chabrol, Pasolini ...*

Lots of Hitchcock. I realized that Léa's character was very similar to Marnie (*Marnie*, 1964). She also has a secret wound that makes her frigid, icy. In the second love scene, where she comes with clenched fists, I asked Samuel to get out of the shot. Suddenly he was too much, I only needed Léa upside down, in the absence of the other that's concentration in oneself. And in the end, even the murmur of the orgasm was too much. I yelled at Léa, "You're dying, you're dying! Die! I don't want to hear another breath!" She died, and it was absolutely beautiful. There had to be nothing left, only a sort of block of solitude abandoned to my gaze. She tensed up inside as if she had had a nightmare. She came without offering herself. That's obviously Marnie.

A different actress had wanted to play the role, but she was too young, too perky. For that role, you needed that something, that overdose of age that makes Léa so touching. I got rid of all the *beauty masks*[50] that they're always using during color correction to smooth out the lines in women's faces *ad aeternam*. Color correctors use them as a matter of routine and, supposedly, they don't distract the eye, but they do erase the pores of the skin. As far as the spectator is concerned, even if you don't know that you're watching skin breathe, you can feel it, and those filters clear away emotion, even on an infinitesimal level. The harshness of a face, wrinkles, it all contributes to its beauty. It's a challenge, because Léa had to be rejuvenated by love, love had to rejuvenate her, give her back the transparency of adolescent eyes.

I hadn't anticipated that you would turn adolescence into a sort of Pasolinian tornado that ravages everything. You eventually make us understand that he is obviously going to emerge unscathed from this experience. He's on a stage, playing out his passions ...

Adolescence is, after all, the ultimate thing. It blows up in your face in the first close-up. I thought Samuel was stunning. That naturalness, that grace, that smile revealing those evenly placed, pearl-white teeth. It was *Girl with a Pearl Earring*. "Young Man with Pearl Teeth." How are you supposed to not fall in love? My assistant said, "I'd love to be in Léa's place," which meant that I had gotten it, that desire flowed from one to the other, they enlightened each other. I filmed Samuel like a girl, like those

---

46. A digital filter, used during color correction, that harmonizes skin texture, erasing the slightest detail that could catch the spectator's eye (pores, wrinkles, dark circles, red patches ...).

painters who paint boys as beautifully as they paint girls. That ambiguity is adolescence's privilege. Lots of people were distraught that Léa would so selfishly shatter Théo's life. But Theo experiences his first heartbreak, that's all. It's like in *Brief Crossing*. As ridiculous as it may seem, that first despair can be fatal. That's what's so beautiful, so incandescent about adolescence. Adolescent suicide, that's a subject I'm passionate about.

In the sex scenes, you feel the need to be modest with your actors, but you still manage to find, inside of that limit, a sort of pictorial necessity.

When I saw the Elastoplast loincloth, I was shocked, really angry. How could they do that to me?

But your actor was a minor!

I don't care, he was of the age of consent! I was petrified. They don't even have any hair on them, those loincloths. Flesh-colored Elastoplast, that's just the worst.

Maybe it's because you talk about it so much, but I've really felt the influence that painting has had on you, much more than before.

It's a way of getting around the loincloth, which always makes movements artificial. The only solution was to tune into the great painters I love. After the first love scene, I had no other choice than to have Samuel sit cross-legged on the bed, and there I was obviously thinking about Caravaggio. For me, Caravaggio paints with a 60 mm lens, with that almost plebian intimacy of faces, very Pasolinian. Obviously, I have fun flirting with *Teorema* (Pier Paolo Pasolini, 1968); Théo is the archangel who eroticizes the entire family. When Samuel first appears, he hangs from the doorframe and swings his hips forward like in the poster for *Accattone* (Pier Paolo Pasolini, 1961)! I said to myself, "He needs to come out of the bathtub soaking wet and she needs to see him unexpectedly." The moment they pass each other had to be choreographed, but the corridor was impossibly narrow. I said to Léa, "Suck your stomach in and hold on to the door handles, that's how he'll be able to pass." That was the only possible solution. You can't cut on paper, you have to find solutions on set, with the details of a specific place serving as anchor points for the actors.

The scene at the lake, when Léa Drucker playfully tries to drown Samuel, is a precipitate of the film: only one or the other can survive.

You can't be afraid of symbols. I strangle all my actors in my films. In this case, first his little sister strangles him, very hard. That's me when I was little, I strangled all the boys in judo. Léa wasn't enjoying drowning Samuel, it's a drive, she's attached to drowning him systematically. All he had to do was not say, "You can't get rid of me!"

It's brilliant, the idea of the little girl who dresses up as a grown woman, who puts on her high heels and lipstick.

The actual little girl who was living in the house where we were shooting came to tell me that her stuffed animals were in the film and that it wasn't right that she wasn't in it, so I found a little role for her. One weekend, she came into the garden with her mother's high heel shoes on. I also felt passionate about the two young adopted girls. There were so many magical takes, irresistible smiles. Saïd restrained me; otherwise, during editing, I would have made a film about the two kids. He was ruthless and he was right. Still, it was like a dagger to the heart, giving up those takes. But it's true that if we had kept them, the relationship between Samuel and Léa would have been stretched too thin, they wouldn't have been as in love with each other.

What makes a good producer, in your opinion?

Saïd is definitely a good producer. He seeks you out to make a film, and he's never wrong about directors or subjects. He leaves you totally alone during the shoot. Then, during the editing process, he locks himself in the editing room with the first cut, what they call "the bear." He takes a look at all of the material and then delivers his verdict like a sledgehammer: "You have enough there to make a great film; figure out a way to find it. You need to cut an hour," and then he'll give his first instructions. At first, you're dazed by what he has to say, but when you go back into the editing room, you realize very quickly that he is generally right and it saves a lot of time. He takes over the film that he had let me make exactly as I had wanted. It becomes his, and he asks me to chisel his diamond, without forgetting a facet. At first, it's minutes, then it's seconds that need to be cut.

The few words that he says sound like orders, when in fact they're not, they're expressions of what he takes for granted in the film. But his lapidary style, essentially, is also the language of editing. He's a great producer, completely passionate. Ready for anything, even ready to hurt me, to take the film even higher.

If I have to challenge him, of course I'll be throwing up all night the night before, but I don't give in. I have a problem with authority, and I've never been able to stand it. That's why my childhood couldn't have been anything other than hell. So it's not in my nature to put up with the outrageous authority that Saïd had. He would cut shots out and if I put them back in, it was a case of high treason. Once, I wrote him a letter at six o'clock in the morning, ten supercharged pages that I didn't even send. Once the crisis had passed, he didn't even want to read it, although it's still an important literary gesture.

He has been as ruthless with me as I am with actors. It's very painful to go through but afterward, we're both so happy! If we were to make another film, the last thing I would want is for him to spare me; the film would take a hit. Lots of people, starting with journalists, think that because cinema is an industry of entertainment and distraction, that you have to be nice and have fun on a shoot. No, we're working. Actors aren't playing, they're working. The ambiguity of language and the televisual mode of talk shows and bloopers have distorted people's understanding of it. We work with determination and passion, from morning until night. And we are all overwhelmed by stage fright and anxiety, the idea that we won't be able to succeed. We all hide our fear, because you have to act as if you're sure of yourself, although we're all mortified by fear and doubt. As long as you don't have the shot, well, you don't have it.

There's that last, slobbery kiss between Samuel and Léa. How did you get your actors to do that?

At one point, I had to overcome my shyness, and take action. I showed Samuel what to do with his lips. He had to let the redness of the mucous membranes show, not really kiss her, no, but instead to drool on her. The drool, the tears, the snot, all of that had to intermingle so that he didn't even know what he was doing anymore, like a lost child. The actors had to be alone in the world. And I wanted that to last, to last, to be interminable. Because it's so beautiful that it should never end. I need to keep seeing it, seeing it again, until I'm satiated ... until Léa says in a dying voice, "Stop!" We had to find a state of sadness in them that transcends morality, that transcends space, a state of irresistible sadness. I said to him, "You're young, and you're going to die of your first love affair. I want you to be on the brink of suicide. I want you to make me cry. Take your time, don't turn away until you have to!" Samuel had to overcome his pride, he had to become Perdican or the young Werther.

The very last love scene in the wood shed is very beautiful, it's the only sex scene that's filmed in a long shot, very "Breillat," very pictorial.

In the screenplay, I had simply written, "And it takes place there, on the floor," with four short lines of romantic dialogue. And so no one in the crew had understood that there was a third real love scene. I tried to tell myself that my two actors wouldn't be naked, but those logs in the shed, those logs that were like actual trunks of murdered trees, were too dreamlike, and I had to do something with them. They were there for me, for my film, like an unexpected opportunity. I mustered up all my courage and I went to tell my two actors that I was very sorry but they had to be naked again ... I'd been imagining the scene all night. Léa's clenched fist, the key in her hand, and the ruggedness of the logs against Samuel's pearlescent body.

That film has an unusual number of love scenes. Gabrièle, my assistant, said that it would take three hours, that it was unexpected, but that it was OK, she'd figure it out. She's incredibly sweet and serene. She always tells me, "Everything's fine, you shoot so quickly." I don't know if that's true. As we had expected, we shot for three hours, in intense concentration and ungodly heat. We rehearsed, we exhausted ourselves rehearsing, and then we did one take after another, with what worked, what didn't, the key in Léa's hand that was so difficult to film. The slightest thing will spoil the imaginary perfection of the shot. At a certain point, you come up with the magical shot, and it's as you never even imagined it would be.

The magical shot arrived at last: Samuel's body with its terrifying whiteness, that stays almost totally still when he's making love. And then, the faces: Léa turns crimson, Samuel nestles his head in her neck. I don't know why, but I told him always to clench Léa as if he were going to smother her. It was beautiful and very moving, and I had never seen Samuel like that before. The face of a Renaissance angel, with an expression of total peace. The closed eyelids, as if he were savoring that infinite seraphic bliss that kept him from opening his eyes. It was breathtaking and I watched, silently, that absolute mystery. We had created a religious tableau, but this time, I hadn't copied anything. That one, I hadn't seen in any museum, it belongs to me. A motionless oeuvre that, nevertheless, breathes ... I said, "Open your eyes, Samuel, try to look up without moving your head." He did it, but struggled to come back to himself. He slowly opened his eyes, his gaze was like a hallucinatory blue flash. That shot is my life's dream. I don't know how we managed to do it.

How did you get the idea to finish the film with a fade to black on the ring?

It was a sudden urge that just came over me. I asked Jeanne to light all of the scenes very brightly, I always want my actors to be seen as if they were in broad daylight, even if it's the middle of the night. But this time, I asked Jeanne to give me a somber, deathly light, for everything to become charcoal gray. Léa comes back into her husband's bedroom, she gets back into bed, snuggles up against him, and says, "Pierre …" He answers, "Be quiet," and then, after the last line, a fade to black going toward total darkness, with the wedding ring glowing. That makes me roar with laughter, I love that! It's the absolute height of cliché, but clichés are always good. The commonplace, that's where we are. It's a place, but it's the place of denial. That's why I was so interested in the screenplay.

He's grateful to her that she lied to him until the end, that she was also capable of doing that out of love.

Yes, you mustn't lance the boil, never, otherwise streams of pus will come pouring out. It's incredibly heavy carrying the weight of a lie, it's very difficult. I carried one for a long time and, even now, I'd like to confess to get some relief. So he says, "Be quiet," and everything will go on in the best of all possible worlds. Actually, when she comes back to bed, Olivier Rabourdin asks, "What was that?" not "Who was that?"

There's the ring, but there's also the bracelet that her husband gives her as a Christmas present, that he closes on her wrist as if it were a handcuff.

It's a real ad for Cartier! Cliché, all the way. I just thought of it when I was filming the scene. It wasn't written in the script, and suddenly I realized that he had to give her a sumptuous gift as if he were the guilty one, and the gift had to be a gorgeous bracelet. I chose the "Juste un clou" model from Cartier, which cost €14,000, and is pretty sadomasochistic: it's a gold handcuff to firmly anchor her to the family unit, the symbol of that happiness that's locked up in itself.

The end of the film reminded me of a gorgeous page from Lady Chatterley's Lover *(1928), where D. H. Lawrence describes the energy that Lady Chatterley gets from her gamekeeper: she comes back to life in his arms, and that newfound vitality allows her to be a better spouse, to take better care of her husband. They improve as a couple because she sleeps with someone else.*

Many people insisted that Léa be punished, that she confess everything to her husband. But that's not my style at all. The more people tell me to punish her, the less I do it, obviously.

"Vertigo isn't the fear of falling, but the fear of the irresistible temptation of the fall. It's so terrible that it would be better to throw yourself into the void to make the fear stop." Weren't you afraid of giving away the keys to the movie when Léa talks about her theory of vertigo?

I always give away the keys to my films! At the beginning of *Perfect Love*, I start with the reconstruction of the murder. Everyone told me that it would be useless to make the film after that, that it ruined the suspense. Well, yeah! The suspense comes with how you get there, how? The engineering of human emotions is so complex, it goes off the rails so easily that it's always a delight to watch very scrupulously how it happens. In *Fat Girl*, Roxane says that she'd like for her mom to die in an accident, which ends up happening. It always amuses me to see that, even if they've been warned, audiences never expect what's going to happen. You can say it and repeat it over and over again, but when it does happen, it's a total surprise.

I was stunned when I heard that Sonic Youth song.

At the Cinematheque in Vienna, I discovered a monograph about my work written by Douglas Keesey, a British scholar. The book was like psychoanalysis, it was fascinating, as if he knew me since I was very little, although I had never met this man. I sent him a short email to tell him how much I liked his book, and he answered that he was very touched and that he knows that Kim Gordon loves my films. Her group that's called Body/Head is actually an homage to my films. We contacted her and she did lots of things for *Last Summer*, she didn't even ask for any money.

The closing credits roll over Léo Ferré's "Vingt ans" (Twenty years old). Didn't that spell things out too much?

No, you can never be too explicit with the prevailing neo-McCarthyism. It shuts up the people who say, "Yes, but he's so young, she shouldn't have succumbed, she's guilty!" Saïd suggested that I use music that would make Léa less severe. But I never use music, I call that dressing. When I'm shooting, I'm so glued to the monitor, I want the image to be so dense that it nearly implodes—otherwise, it's shit. So music is excluded from the get-go, since the image is already heavy on its own. On the other hand, ever since *Lost Highway* (David Lynch, 1997), I've often used sub-bass. Ferré's song is about Léa and all of us. Samuel experiences his first magnificent love affair. Of course, he'll be shattered, but he'll pull himself together again. It's not a tragedy if this boy's first love affair doesn't last for a hundred years. It's like Delphine in *36 fillette*, she laughs in the audience's face.

You're totally on her side, you want her to protect the only thing she has left, her family. She is very clear: she'll go to extremes to save it, and that's very understandable. Older people have nothing but that, they have their family.

Conjugal love is beautiful, even if it's boring. Love can be devastating, but there's another kind that's calm and reassuring. The devastating kind of love will never make you happy, it's too fiery. It has to break up eventually.

Which of the two kinds of love is more desirable?

The most beneficial kind for composing works of art is being madly in love, it elicits tons of thoughts, tons of dreams, it carries you away into idealism—and we need idealism. I prefer falling in love, being ridiculous and playing the martyr, to being cynical. I prefer to be madly in love, but it is a kind of madness. You have to understand that: you're young and naive, incandescent with bliss, and then one day, you're miserable, you think that you'll never recover. But you end up recovering, even if it takes time.

The teenager will bounce back, he just can't know that because he's in pain. But what about her? Can older people bounce back?

No one cares if old people are unhappy. Humanity is merciless, it's only for the young. If they're unhappy, everyone's unhappy. But old people, no one cares. When you're seventeen, love is something you take hold of and then throw away, that's the truth. He at least learned about the gravity and beauty of things. It's an initiation.

Where does the film stand, for you?

In necessity, in those problems that you solve, notably the fact that I couldn't find my ending. When you start working on a film, you don't know what you want to say, it's very fluid. The screenplay is clear, but then human flesh intrudes and makes everything much more complex. Why does the scene in the woodshed at the end mean so much to me? I saw, there, that something was happening that was my life's dream. And I transformed the film into a love story. It wasn't written or planned— Léa and Samuel led me to it because they had a luminous relationship. All I had to do was embroider around the edges, exaggerate a bit …

What is that dream?

It's experiencing *jouissance* as an ecstasy, with that ultra-white body at the start. They do practically nothing. That's fusion, that's ecstasy: a vibratory stillness that reaches a sort of bliss and carnal fusion. That's making love. They're not fucking, they're making love, it's a very different thing.

What are you going to work on now?

Yesterday, I told Saïd Ben Saïd that we had to talk about our future together. Before he contacted me, I had written a commissioned screenplay based on a book called *N'oublie pas que je t'aime* (Don't forget that I love you). It's exactly like *Love Story* (Arthur Hiller, 1970), except that it's a true story, and that really interests me. I adore romances, you have no idea how romantic I am. Saïd will definitely find something to pitch to me, I've already turned down two projects, and he certainly understands that I can't do everything. I'm not a skilled director. Skillfulness is the worst part of art, by the way. I also sent him an idea about the death of the Duke of Bourbon, it's very, very interesting, I have the entire transcript of the trial, but I'd have to do it as a Netflix series.

You're going to end up on Netflix?

I told him that I didn't necessarily want to make it myself, but I could at least pilot the project.

I think that you should do your own projects first. You shouldn't write for other people.

You think? It's true that I'm too old, I need to work only on films that are really essential. I still have a lot of stories to tell. My first boyfriend, when I was twelve. My relationships with my mother, my sister … lots of things. Everything is interesting in detail, when you know how to look. *A Woman like Satan* (Julien Duvivier, 1959) … and then the story of a girl I caught on Change.org who said that she had been raped and her rapist hadn't come to trial after six years. I wrote to her, I have her whole story, a very complicated one. There's also the story of Asia Argento and Weinstein, which really interests me! Essentially, it's a public story, it wouldn't be about her anymore, but me. I think I even have the script in my computer under the title "MeToo, She Said."

Where are you off to now?

To Portugal, I need to be there for the work to start. That's where I prefer to be, I have a beautiful house, with marble bathrooms, marble benches. Not those hideous benches for invalids.

Do you miss not being there?

I miss the life I love there, but I'd rather be making films, even though I've always hated getting up early, even to go to school. I'm a night owl.

What time do you go to bed?

I don't sleep very much. I wondered if I was going to be able to hang on during the shoot. I found that Léo Ferré song, "Vingt Ans," in the middle of the night. It was perfect for the film, perfect for those angry people who don't understand that when you're twenty, you're brazen. I was a very brazen young girl, nothing scared me, except for virginity, except for undressing, except for coming on to boys. I liked people to come on to me and I love that tipping point, when you move from being clothed to being naked. It's extravagant, that passage … a sort of immediate intimacy that has always fascinated me. I'm so interested in seeing how that happens, just that.

The astonishment of being undressed.

Undressing, penetrating … It seemed impossible in everyday life to be penetrated. And yet it's so simple, so natural—it happens in a flash. Tipping over into another reality.

Don't hesitate to let me know if there are any topics you'd like to address that we've missed. I'll be going over this all month …

And you'll see that this book is going to be like my film that was three hours long, which was a disaster because I didn't know what film I had made. I was traumatized. I couldn't find the answer. What is the film about? What story does it tell?

FILMS BY CATHERINE BREILLAT

A Real Young Girl (*Une vraie jeune fille*)
France | 1975 | 93 min.

Director: Catherine Breillat
Screenplay: Catherine Breillat, based on her novel *Le soupirail*
Production companies: CB Films (Catherine Breillat Films), Artedis (Paris), La Boétie Films
Producers: André Génovès, Daniel Daërt
Executive producer: Pierre-Richard Muller
Original distributor: Rezo Films (Paris)
Director of photography: Pierre Fattori
Camera operator: Patrick Godaert
Sound engineer: Bernard Mangière
Original music: Mort Shuman
Original songwriter: Catherine Breillat
Sets: Catherine Breillat
Costumes: Catherine Breillat
Makeup: Catherine Breillat
Editing: Annie Charrier
Cast: Charlotte Alexandra (Alice Bonnard), Hiram Keller (Pierre-Evariste Renard, aka Jim), Rita Maiden (Alice's mother), Bruno Balp (Alice's father), Georges Guéret (Martial), Shirley Stoler (the grocer)

Nocturnal Uproar (*Tapage nocturne*)
France | 1979 | 94 min.

Director: Catherine Breillat
Screenplay: Catherine Breillat, based on her novel *Tapage nocturne*
Production companies: Axe Films, French Productions
Executive producer: Pierre Sayag
Associate producer: Guy Belfond
Original distributor: Gaumont Distribution
Director of photography: Jacques Boumendil
Sound engineer: Alain Curvelier

Original music: Serge Gainsbourg
Sets: Pierre Audouard, Dominique Antony
Costumes: Sylvie Gautrelet
Makeup: Jacqueline Pipard
Editing: Annie Charrier, Claudio Ventura
Cast: Dominique Laffin (Solange), Marie-Hélène Breillat (Emmanuelle), Bertrand Bonvoisin (Bruno), Joe Dallesandro (Jim), Dominique Basquin (Dorothée), Daniel Langlet (Bruel), Bruno Grimaldi (Frédéric), Bruno Devoldère (the husband), Maud Rayer (Léna), Hubert Drac (the director), Annie Charrier (Annie), Gérard Lanvin (the guy)

36 fillette
France | 1987 | 88 min.

Director: Catherine Breillat
Screenplay: Catherine Breillat, based on her novel 36 fillette
Production companies: French Productions, CB Films (Catherine Breillat Films), CFC (Compagnie Française Cinématographique)
Producers: Emmanuel Schlumberger, Valérie Seydoux
Executive producer: Pierre Sayag
Original distributor: Gaumont Distribution
Director of photography: Laurent Dailland
Sound engineers: Jean Minondo, Michel Barlier, Julien Cloquet
Mixing: Dominique Dalmasso
Sets: Olivier Paultre
Costumes: Valérie Seydoux
Editing: Yann Dedet
Cast: Delphine Zentout (Lili), Étienne Chicot (Maurice), Olivier Parnière (Bertrand), Jean-Pierre Léaud (Boris Golovine), Berta Domínguez D. (Anne-Marie), Jean-François Stévenin (the father), Diane Bellego (Georgia), Stéphane Moquet (Gi-Pé), Adrienne Bonnet (the mother), Cécile Henry (Laetitia), Michel Scotto di Carlo (Stéphane), Anny Chasson (Ms. Weber), Jean-Claude Binoche (Mr. Weber)

Dirty like an Angel (*Sale comme un ange*)
France | 1991 | 105 min.

Screenplay and direction: Catherine Breillat
Production companies: French Productions, CB Films (Catherine Breillat Films), Ciné Manufacture (Paris), Veranfilm
Associate producers: Nella Banfi, Robert Boner, Alessandro Verdecchi
Producer: Emmanuel Schlumberger
Executive producer: Pierre Sayag
Original distributor: Pyramide Distribution (Paris)
Director of photography: Laurent Dailland
Sound engineer: Georges Prat
Mixing: Dominique Dalmasso
Original music: Olivier Manoury
Sets: Olivier Paultre
Costumes: Malika Brahim
Makeup: Muriel Baurens
Editing: Agnès Guillemot
Cast: Claude Brasseur (l'inspecteur Georges Deblache), Lio (Barbara Théron), Nils Tavernier (Didier Théron), Roland Amstutz (the Detective), Claude-Jean Philippe (Mannoni), Léa Gabrielle (Judy), Anny Chasson (Vishia), Lorella Di Cicco (Arlette), Alain Schlumberger (Jeannot), Rénos Mandis (Mohamed), Franck Karoui (Francky), Leila Samir (the Arab Dancer)

Aux Niçois qui mal y pensent
A short for the collective film *À propos de Nice, la suite*
France | 1995 | 22 min.

Screenplay and direction: Catherine Breillat
Production companies: Margo Cinéma, La Sept Cinéma
Producer: François Margolin
Director of photography: Laurent Dailland
Sound engineer: Jean Minondo
Editing: Katya Chelli
Cast: Yvette Wojtak-Boisson, Robert Benassayag, Marie-Jeanne Meillan

Perfect Love (*Parfait amour!*)
France | 1996 | 113 min.

Screenplay and direction: Catherine Breillat
Production companies: Dacia Films, CB Films (Catherine Breillat Films), La Sept Cinéma
Producer: Georges Benayoun
Executive producer: Françoise Guglielmi
Director of photography: Laurent Dailland
Sound engineer: Jean Minondo
Mixing: François Sempé
Sets: Françoise Dupertuis
Costumes: Cécile Cotten, Catherine Breillat
Makeup: Claire Monatte
Editing: Agnès Guillemot
Cast: Francis Renaud (Christophe), Isabelle Renauld (Frédérique), Laura Saglio (Emmanuelle), Alain Soral (Philippe), Delphine de Malherbe (Valérie de La Tournelle), Serge Toubiana (Louis), Coralie Gengenbach (Bénédicte), Marie Lebée (the judge), Alice Mitterrand (Wanda), Michèle Rème (Christophe's mother), Tom Rocheteau (Vincent)

Romance
France | 1999 | 98 min.

Screenplay and direction: Catherine Breillat
Production companies: Flach Film (Paris), CB Films (Catherine Breillat Films), ARTE France Cinéma
Producer: Jean-François Lepetit
Executive producer: Catherine Jacques
Original distributor: Rezo Films (Paris)
Director of photography: Yorgos Arvanitis
Sound engineer: Paul Lainé
Mixing: Éric Bonnard
Original music: DJ Valentin, Raphaël Tidas
Art direction: Frédérique Belvaux
Sets: Pierre Gerbaux, Alexis Forestier, Julien Poitou-Weber

Costumes: Anne Dunsford-Varenne, Christian Lacroix, Catherine Breillat
Makeup: Claire Monatte
Editing: Agnès Guillemot
Cast: Caroline Ducey (Marie), Sagamore Stévenin (Paul), François Berléand (Robert, the school principal), Rocco Siffredi (Paolo), Reza Habouhossein (Man on stairs), Fabien de Jomaron (Claude), Emma Colberti (Charlotte), Ashley Wanninger (Ashley)

Fat Girl (*À ma soeur!*)
France-Italy | 2000 | 93 min.

Screenplay and direction: Catherine Breillat
Production companies: Flach Film (Paris), CB Films (Catherine Breillat Films), ARTE France Cinéma, Immagine e Cinema (Rome), Urania Pictures (Rome)
Producer: Jean-François Lepetit
Production manager: Fredy Lagrost
Original distributor: Rezo Films (Paris)
Directors of photography: Yorgos Arvanitis, Olivier Fortin, Christophe Le Caro
Sound engineers: Jean Minondo, Olivier Villette, Erwan Kerzanet
Mixing: Vincent Arnardi, Salim Amrani
Original music: Catherine Breillat, "Moi, je m'ennuie," "J'ai mis mon cœur à pourrir"
Sets: François-Renaud Labarthe, Yann Richard, Cécilia Blom, Fabienne David, Christophe Graziani, Fabrice Héraud, Gérald Lemaire, Jean-Luc Molle
Costumes: Catherine Meillan, Sanine Schlumberger, Anne Dunsford-Varenne, Janet Latimer
Makeup: Claire Monatte, Monique Kaiser
Editing: Pascale Chavance, Gwenola Heaulme, Frédéric Barbe
Cast: Anaïs Reboux (Anaïs), Roxane Mesquida (Elena), Libero De Rienzo (Fernando), Arsinée Khanjian (the mother), Romain Goupil (the father), Laura Betti (Fernando's mother), Albert Goldberg (the killer), Odette Barrière (friend at residence), Anne Matthijsse (friend at residence), Pierre Renverseau (friend at residence), Jean-Marc Boulanger

(friend at residence), Frédérick Bodin (the waiter), Michel Guillemin (janitor), Josette Cathalan (the saleswoman), Claude Sese (the police officer), Marc Samuel (inspector)

Brief Crossing (*Brève traversée*)
France | 2001 | 84 min.

Screenplay and direction: Catherine Breillat
Production companies: ARTE France Unité Fictions, GMT Productions (Paris)
Producers: Jean-Pierre Guérin, Pierre Eid, Christophe Valette
Director of photography: Eric Gautier
Sound engineer: Yves Osmu
Mixing: Vincent Arnardi
Sets: Frédérique Belvaux
Makeup: Claire Monatte
Editing: Pascale Chavance
Cast: Sarah Pratt (Alice), Gilles Guillain (Thomas), Christelle Dacosta (la douanière France), Alexandre Le Balidec (French custum oficer), Jean-Claude Cavelier (the night-club waiter), Franck Lemaître (the night-club waiter), Marc Jablonski (the cook), Marc Filippi (the magician), Nicholas Hawtrey (le old Englishman), Philippe Quaisse (the photographer)

Sex Is Comedy
France | 2002 | 93 min.

Screenplay and direction: Catherine Breillat
Production companies: Flach Film (Paris), CB Films (Catherine Breillat Films)
Coproduction: ARTE France Cinéma
Producer: Jean-François Lepetit
Associate producer: António da Cunha Telles
Original distributor: Rezo Films (Paris)
Directors of photography: Laurent Machuel, Benoît Rizzotti, Tiago Nuno Silva, Nuno Relvas, Bruno Ramos, Yorgos Arvanitis

Sound engineers: Yves Osmu, Yves Lévêque, Filipe Gonçalves, Jean Minondo
Mixing: Emmanuel Croset, Laure Arto
Costumes: Valérie Guégan, Rute Correia, Betty Martins, Sanine Schlumberger
Makeup: Dominique Colladant, Ana Lorena, Claire Monatte
Editing: Pascale Chavance, Sylvain Dupuy, Pedro Marques
Cast: Anne Parillaud (Jeanne), Grégoire Colin (the actor), Roxane Mesquida (the actress), Ashley Wanninger (Léo), Dominique Colladant (Willy), Bart Binnema (the director of photography), Yves Osmu (the sound engineer), Francis Seleck (the production manager), Elisabete Piecho (the continuity girl), Diane Scapa (the production designer), Ana Lorena (a makeup artist), Claire Monatte (a makeup artist), Arnaldo Junior (the chief electrician), Elisabete Silva (the boom operator), Júlia Fragata (the set dresser)

Anatomy of Hell (*Anatomie de l'enfer*)
France | 2004 | 100 min.

Director: Catherine Breillat
Screenplay: Catherine Breillat, based on her novel Pornocracy
Production companies: Flach Film (Paris), CB Films (Catherine Breillat Films)
Producer: Jean-François Lepetit
Executive producer: António da Cunha Telles
Original distributor: Rezo Films (Paris)
Directors of photography: Yorgos Arvanitis, Guillaume Schiffman, Miguel Malheiros, Susana Gomes
Sound engineers: Carlos Pinto, Filipe Gonçalves
Mixing: Emmanuel Croset
Sets: Pedro Sá Santos, Jean-Marie Milon, Paula Szabo, Pedro Garcia
Costumes: Valérie Guégan, Betty Martins, Catherine Meillan, Sanine Schlumberger
Makeup: Ana Lorena
Editing: Pascale Chavance, Frédéric Barbe
Cast: Amira Casar (the woman), Rocco Siffredi (the man), Alexandre Belin (blow-job lover 1), Manuel Taglang (blow-job lover 2), Jacques

Monge (man in bar), Claudio Carvalho (l'enfant oiseau), Carolina Lopes (the little girl), Diogo Rodriques (a little boy), João Marques (a little boy), Bruno Fernandes (a little boy), Maria Edite Moreira (a pharmacist), Maria João Santos (a pharmacist), Catherine Breillat (the narrator's voice)

The Last Mistress (*Une vieille maîtresse*)
France-Italy | 2007 | 114 min.

Director: Catherine Breillat
Screenplay: Catherine Breillat, based on the novel Une vieille maîtresse by Barbey d'Aurevilly
Production companies: Flach Film (Paris), CB Films (Catherine Breillat Films)
Producer: Jean-François Lepetit
Original distributor: StudioCanal
Director of photography: Yorgos Arvanitis
Sound engineers: Yves Osmu, Yves Lévêque, Sylvain Lasseur, Roland Duboué, Emmanuel Croset
Sets: François-Renaud Labarthe
Costumes: Anaïs Romand
Editing: Pascale Chavance
Cast: Asia Argento (Vellini), Fu'ad Aït Aattou (Ryno de Marigny), Roxane Mesquida (Hermangarde de Polastron), Claude Sarraute (the Marquise de Flers), Yolande Moreau (the Countess d'Artelles), Michael Lonsdale (the Viscount de Prony), Anne Parillaud (Mme de Solcy), Jean-Philippe Tessé (the Viscount de Mareuil), Sarah Pratt (the Countess de Mendoze), Amira Casar (Mademoiselle Marie-Cornélie Falcon), Lio (la Chanteuse), Isabelle Renauld (l'Arrogante), Léa Seydoux (Olivia)

Bluebeard (*Barbe bleue*)
France | 2009 | 90 min.

Director: Catherine Breillat
Screenplay: Catherine Breillat, based on the folktale "Bluebeard" by Charles Perrault

Production companies: Flach Film (Paris), CB Films (Catherine Breillat Films), ARTE France Cinéma
Producers: Sylvette Frydman, Jean-François Lepetit
Director of photography: Vilko Filač
Sound engineers: Yves Osmu, Stéphane Brunclair, Éric Bonnard
Sets: Olivier Jacquet
Costumes: Rose-Marie Melka
Makeup: Claire Monnatte
Editing: Pascale Chavance
Cast: Dominique Thomas (Bluebeard), Lola Créton (Marie-Catherine), Daphné Baiwir (Anne), Lola Giovannetti (Marie-Anne), Farida Khelfa (the Mother Superior)

The Sleeping Beauty (*La belle endormie*)
France | 2010 | 90 min.

Director: Catherine Breillat
Screenplay: Catherine Breillat, based on the folktale "The Sleeping Beauty" by Charles Perrault
Production companies: Flach Film, CB Films (Catherine Breillat Films), ARTE France
Producers: Sylvette Frydman, Jean-François Lepetit
Director of photography: Denis Lenoir
Sound engineers: Emmanuel Croset, Sébastien Noiré, Yves Osmu
Sets: François-Renaud Labarthe
Costumes: Rose-Marie Melka
Editing: Pascale Chavance
Cast: Carla Besnaïnou (Anastasia at ten years old), Julia Artamonov (Anastasia at sixteen years old), Kerian Mayan (Peter), David Chausse (Johan), Luna Charpentier (la petite brigande), Rhizlaine El Cohen (la brigande adulte), Delia Bouglione-Romanès (la chanteuse tsigane), Diana Rudychenko (Véroutchka), Maricha Lopoukhine (the grandmother), Jean-Philippe Tessé (the father), Odile Mallet (la fée Carabosse), Dounia Sichov (la fée aînée), Leslie Lipkins (la fée puînée), Rosine Favey (une vieille mégère), Dominique Hulin (Giant), Laurine David (Princess), Marie Piton (Johan's mother), Pierre Estorges (le chef de gare), Camille Chalons

(la fée cadette), Romane Portail (the Snow Queen), Anne-Lise Kedvès (Peter's mother)

Abuse of Weakness (*Abus de faiblesse*)
France-Germany-Belgium | 2012 | 104 min.

Director: Catherine Breillat
Screenplay: Catherine Breillat, based on her book Abus de faiblesse, coauthored with Jean-François Kervéan
Production companies: Flach Film (Paris), Iris Films, Iris Productions Deutschland GmbH (Munich), CB Films (Catherine Breillat Films), ARTE France Cinéma, uMedia (Brussels)
Producers: Jean-François Lepetit, Nicolas Steil, Jesus Gonzalez
Original distributor: Rezo Films (Paris)
Director of photography: Alain Marcoen
Sound engineers: Dominique Warnier, Julie Brenta, Benoît Biral
Original music: Didier Lockwood
Sets: Pierre-François Limbosch
Costumes: Catherine Breillat, François Jugé
Editing: Pascale Chavance
Cast: Isabelle Huppert (Maud), Kool Shen (Vilko), Laurence Ursino (Andy), Christophe Sermet (Ezzé), Ronald Leclercq (Gino), Tristan Schotte (Antoine), Daphné Baiwir (Hortense), Dimitri Tomsej (Louis), Nicolas Steil (Louis's father), Jean-François Lepetit (Jean-Paul), Marc de Bodin de Galembert (the lawyer), Patrick Van Ackere (le kiné), François Stockmans (le professeur), Fred LeBelge (le journaliste interviewer), Valérie Chavet (l'orthophoniste), Ismaël Villar Bonilla (l'ambulancier), Valérie Azura (l'attachée de presse), Axelle Beerens (l'orthopédiste), Andrée Cambier (Grane), Jean-Pierre Denuit (l'huissier), Catherine Breillat (a hospital patient)

Last Summer (*L'été dernier*)
France | 2023 | 104 min.

Director: Catherine Breillat
Screenplay: Catherine Breillat, in collaboration with Pascal Bonitzer, based on the film Queen of Hearts, written by Maren Louise Kaëhne and May el-Toukhy, and directed by May el-Toukhy
Production company: SBS Productions
Producers: Saïd Ben Saïd, Caroline Blanco, René Ezra, Clifford Werber
Distributor: Pyramide Distribution
Director of photography: Jeanne Lapoirie
Sound engineers: Damien Luquet, Loïc Prian
Mixing: Cyril Holtz
Musical collaboration: Kim Gordon
Sets: Sébastien Danos
Costumes: Khadija Zeggaï
Makeup: Delphine Jaffart
Editing: François Quiqueré
Cast: Léa Drucker (Anne), Samuel Kircher (Théo), Olivier Rabourdin (Pierre), Clotilde Courau (Mina), Serena Hu (Serena), Angela Chen (Angela), Jérôme Kircher (l'ami d'Anne et Pierre)

ABOUT THE AUTHORS

Catherine Breillat is a filmmaker and writer based in Paris. She is known not only for her films focusing on themes of sexuality but also for her best-selling novels.

Murielle Joudet is a film critic for *Le Monde*, as well as for TV and radio. She is the author of *Isabelle Huppert: Vivre ne nous regarde pas* (2018), *Gena Rowlands: On aurait dû dormir* (2020), and *La Seconde Femme: Ce que les actrices font à la vieillesse* (2022).